The Poetry Remedy

VIKING

The Poetry Remedy

Prescriptions for the Heart, Mind, and Soul

····································
····································
····································

WILLIAM SIEGHART

VIKING

VIKING
An imprint of Penguin Random House LLC
penguinrandomhouse.com

First published under the title *The Poetry Pharmacy* in Great Britain by
Particular Books (UK) 2017
This expanded edition published by Viking,
an imprint of Penguin Random House LLC 2019

Editorial material and selection copyright © 2017,
2019 by William Sieghart

The acknowledgments on pp. 189–196 constitutes an
extension of this copyright page.

LIBRARY OF CONGRESS CATALOGING-IN-PUBLICATION DATA
Names: Sieghart, William, 1960– editor.
Title: The poetry remedy: prescriptions for the heart, mind, and soul /
edited by William Sieghart.
Description: New York: Viking, 2019. | "First published in
Great Britain by Particular Books (UK) 2017"— Verso title page. |
Identifiers: LCCN 2019005763 (print) | LCCN 2019013702 (ebook) |
ISBN 9780525561095 (ebook) | ISBN 9780525561088 (hardcover)
Subjects: LCSH: Happiness—Poetry. | Inspiration—Poetry. | Hope—Poetry. |
Adjustment (Psychology)—Poetry. | Self-actualization (Psychology)—Poetry. |
Conduct of life—Poetry. | BISAC: POETRY / Anthologies (multiple authors). |
SELF-HELP / Personal Growth / Happiness. | POETRY / Inspirational & Religious.
Classification: LCC PN6110.H14 (ebook) | LCC PN6110.H14 P64 2019
(print) | DDC 808.81—dc23
LC record available at https://lccn.loc.gov/2019005763

Printed in Canada
1   3   5   7   9   10   8   6   4   2

Designed by Amanda Dewey

To Felicity Sieghart, in her ninety-second year

CONTENTS

Motivations

Self-Image and Self-Acceptance

The World and Other People

Love and Loss

With Thanks

To Evie Prichard, my helper in this project, who will one day have many books to her name and whose part in this book has been extraordinary.

To Jenny Dyson, who created the Poetry Pharmacy in the first place.

To Elizabeth Sheinkman, my agent, who conceived the book and made it happen.

To my editor, Donald Futers, and to everyone at Penguin for their wonderful contributions.

To Susannah Herbert, Jane Davies, Neil Astley, Jeanette Winterson, and all the anthologists who helped me in my selection.

INTRODUCTION

You don't need to be a poet to find solace in poetry.

I was eight years old when I was first sent to boarding school, and I was desperately unhappy. At a time when friends were in short supply, I found that poetry became my friend. Reading it aloud was the only thing I was good at—I even won a prize or two doing it. That, I think, began my whole relationship with poetry.

Since then, these careful crystallizations of feeling, thought, and experience have been a loyal and generous companion to me, even in the most difficult of times. Again and again, in my loneliest hours and in my most tumultuous, I have discovered the greatest solace in finding, reading, and sometimes memorizing the perfect poem for the moment.

As a young adult, I was about to cross a road in London when the lights changed. A man standing next to me stepped out into the path of a car and was immediately run down. The suddenness of it all was incredible: the next thing I knew, he was lying on the road, unconscious. Somebody from the crowd was giving him mouth-to-mouth resuscitation and had asked for my help pummeling the poor man's heart back to life.

He was lucky. By some incredible fluke, an ambulance was there in a matter of minutes. The man's heart started beating again, the police took my statement, and off he sped, leaving me standing uselessly on the same street corner with the traffic flowing by. Life went on as it had before. The only evidence of this extraordinary drama was my hands, still covered with blood. As I slowly got my breath back, I remembered a poem I'd learned of Philip Larkin's. It's called "Ambulances," and it's about the drama and anguish we go through when situations like this arise; how seeing an ambulance brings the dread we feel about the future into greater focus, and "dulls to distance all we are." Between those apt words and the strong drink I immediately sought out, I was helped to process what had been a bizarre, unexpected, and very destabilizing two hours.

That particular poem didn't make it into this book, in the end. But what it did for me in that moment points to something much more universal. Like that isolated eight-year-old, or that quaking young man, a great many of us turn to poetry in times of need. Above all, when we're grieving, when we're brokenhearted, and when we find ourselves struggling to understand the things we're feeling, we long for the *connection* poetry can provide. To find the right poem at that crucial moment, one capable of expressing our situation with considerably more elegance than we can ourselves, is to discover a powerful sense of complicity, and that precious realization: *I'm not the only one who feels like this.*

In the words of Alan Bennett, "The best moments in reading are when you come across something—a thought, a feeling, a way of looking at things—which you had thought special and particular to you. Now here it is, set down by someone else, a person you have never met, someone even who is long dead. And it is as if a hand has come out, and taken yours."

The problem is shared. More than that, very often, it is transformed: the poet has made what you're going through seem more intriguing, more timeless, and more valid in some way, and that can be a great comfort. The distance afforded by seeing one's own emotions formalized and made beautiful combines with the visceral connection one feels with this poet, this stranger, who *understands*, and what results is a sort of peace.

This idea, that there can be a therapeutic power to a poem, is at the heart of *The Poetry Remedy*. But that therapeutic power only exists if you can find the right poem for the right state of mind. This book aims to help by gathering poems that I know from experience will help people through most conceivable difficulties of day-to-day life: through the various faces and frustrations of love, grief, work, and all the other concerns that dominate our thoughts.

There isn't a singular poem for anything, just as there is no singular human response to an emotion. The first breath of love is very different from the last anguished cries of loss. Love has many moods and many stages, just as do regret, and life, and solitude. However momentary or enduring it might be, my hope is that you will find a poem within this book that fits your need.

THE HISTORY OF THE POETRY PHARMACY

I've always believed in the power of poetry to explain people to themselves. In this volume, on page 47, is a poem by Stuart Henson called "The Price." It's the kind of poem that has enormous impact and power, especially when encountered unexpectedly. More than twenty years ago now, I used to post it around London at the height of the windows in the double-decker buses. I'd put it underneath bridges, where I knew buses would have to come to a halt at traffic. It was almost a guerrilla tactic—confronting people with a poem that I knew would startle them, but that I was also confident might help them in some way.

Although I didn't think of it that way at the time, that may well have been the first incarnation of what I came to call the Poetry Pharmacy, the project upon which this book is based. The Pharmacy proper began much later, while I was being interviewed at a literary festival in Cornwall, England, about a more traditional anthology I'd just brought out. A friend of mine, Jenny Dyson, had the idea of allowing me to prescribe poems from that book to audience members after the talk. She set me up in a tent, with two armchairs and a prescription pad. It turned out to be all I needed. The hour we had originally planned for came and went, and then a second, and a third, until many hours later I was still in there, with lines of people still waiting for their appointments.

I realized that we were onto something. Suffering is the access point to poetry for a lot of people: that's when they open their ears, hearts, and minds. Being there with the right words for someone in that moment—when something's happened, when they're in need—is a great comfort, and sometimes creates a love of poetry that can last a lifetime.

After Cornwall, I brought the Poetry Pharmacy to BBC Radio 4. I was asked back to do it again at Christmas—one of the most stressful times of year, as we all know—and then to BBC television, and into the pages of *The Guardian* newspaper. Meanwhile, I never stopped doing my personal consultations. I toured the country, offering Poetry Pharmacies in libraries and festivals. In all of this, I learned how much most people's heartaches have in common. The objects and their circumstances might change, but there's nothing like listening to people's problems in leafy Kensington and then a council estate in Liverpool for making you realize the basic spiritual sameness that runs throughout humanity.

I must have listened, over the last few years, to nearly a thousand people's problems. This book is therefore a compilation of the prescriptions that work, for seventy-four of the problems that really matter. I've found that some of my prescriptions, such as the Hafiz poem you'll read about on p. 33, so inspire people that they seem to leave their chair a foot taller than when they sat down. Seeing the difference the right poem can make written on that many faces has given me confidence in poetry's power to change lives.

HOW TO READ A POEM

People are always telling me that they worry about their ability to read a poem. They don't really know how to. It's almost as though when they're faced with a poem they're instantly intimidated, even though, of course, they can read and write like the best of us.

When I'm asked for tips, I always give the same advice. Don't read the poem like you would a newspaper or a novel. Read it almost like a prayer. Say it aloud in your head as if you're speaking it to somebody else—somebody interested, who makes you want to perform it properly. Or, truly read it out loud if you want to, and if you're not on the bus. Either way, it's the reading aloud that will allow you to properly *hear* it; that will make you understand the rhythms, cadences, and musicality of the words and phrases.

When people tell me they don't understand poetry, I have another recommendation. I tell them to read the same poem night after night. Keep it by your bed, and read it before you switch out the lights. Read it five nights in a row, and you'll find you discover a totally new flavor and feeling from it every time. How you experience a poem depends on your own inner rhythms: what you've been through and what your mood is that day. But more than that, a really good poem is layered. It uncovers itself bit by bit by bit, never finished but always rewarding.

That's why the joy of a really concise and brilliant poem is that you get more out of it every time.

Read the poems in this book however you like. Keep them in your desk drawer for when you feel shaky, or memorize them so you always have them on hand. Read them in the bathtub until the pages are crinkled beyond repair. But however this book works for you, remember that no poem deserves only a single visit. Come back, try again, approach them in a new frame of mind or with a new openness. If you persevere, you may be surprised at how many new friends you make.

The Poetry Remedy

Mental and Emotional Well-being

Condition | Anxiety

Also suitable for: FEAR FOR CHILDREN • FEAR FOR THE
FUTURE • SLEEPLESSNESS • STRESS • WORRYING

For as long as anxiety has existed, human beings have woken up panicking in the night. And anxiety has existed for a long time: at the very least, since we first became aware of ourselves and of the future, however many millennia ago. Yet it was not until the modern age that anxiety seemed to become an epidemic. Ironically, in a time of greater plenty, health, and comfort worldwide than ever before, we are more racked by worry than we have ever been.

No one tells you when you become a parent that you are condemned to worry for the rest of your life. Lying awake at night is usually the worst of all: the blank space of the darkness provides a theater for the most intense and unlikely of worries, putting your sense of powerlessness, of your own vulnerability and of the vulnerabilities of your loved ones, into even sharper perspective. The nighttime is when there is nothing to be done except brood.

These nocturnal concerns are not easy to escape, but I find the calming words of Wendell Berry's "The Peace of Wild Things" help me put things into perspective. Although I live in the middle of a city, far away from the wood drake and the great heron, I can see them in my mind's eye when I whisper his words. Perhaps it is the poetic equivalent of counting sheep, but this poem helps me to calm my mind and my breathing, and drift into unconsciousness.

THE PEACE OF WILD THINGS
Wendell Berry

When despair for the world grows in me
and I wake in the night at the least sound
in fear of what my life and children's lives may be,
I go and lie down where the wood drake
rests in his beauty on the water, and the great heron feeds.
I come into the peace of wild things
who do not tax their lives with forethought
of grief. I come into the presence of still water.
And I feel above me the day-blind stars
waiting with their light. For a time
I rest in the grace of the world, and am free.

Condition | Compulsive Behavior

Also suitable for: ADDICTION • OBSESSION •
SELF-DESTRUCTIVENESS

It's a sad fact that when people are having trouble coping, they often turn to solutions even more destructive than their feelings. Whether they struggle with a drug addiction or simply a propensity to pop over to McDonald's after a hard day, I'm constantly speaking to those who no longer feel in control. I also meet people who have suffered at the hands of others' bad habits, or who have even been subjected to abuse, and who therefore feel that their minds are no longer entirely their own.

It can be hard to imagine changing oneself in the face of pressures like this. When you can't envision a world without a destructive habit, or thoughts that tear you down, that lack of hope can make it even harder to move on. There's nothing more frightening than feeling trapped in a prison of one's own mind and compulsions.

I like the solution offered by these lines by Susan Coolidge because it's straightforward. "OK," they say, "things have been bad. They may be bad again; they may not. In the meantime, let's take heart with the day. Let's begin again and see what happens." It doesn't need to be dramatic, this change in outlook. It's about acceptance, low-level optimism, and incremental change. There's a wisdom to the way so many of our modern-day mantras focus on living in the moment, relishing the now, and smelling the roses; and there's a reason that Alcoholics Anonymous recommends recovery be approached one day at a time. Breaking things down into bite-size chunks doesn't just make them more manageable: it also provides us with many more chances to start again if we fail. This poem urges us to appreciate the fresh beginnings that every day brings with it. But we don't need to stop there. After all, if tomorrow can be the first day of the rest of your life, why not make this very second its first *moment*?

from NEW EVERY MORNING
Susan Coolidge

Every day is a fresh beginning;
    Listen, my soul, to the glad refrain,
And, spite of old sorrow and older sinning,
    And puzzles forecasted and possible pain,
    Take heart with the day, and begin again.

Condition | Depression

Also suitable for: HOPELESSNESS • INTRACTABLE MISERY

The difficulty with depression is that it can make you believe some very illogical things. Once it has its hooks into you, you can end up feeling like you'll never pull yourself free without unraveling completely. There's no escape, you tell yourself. This is just who you are now; this is how you'll feel from now on.

Of course, nothing could be further from the truth. Time and again, in my life and the lives of my patients, I have seen these wonderful, transformative moments that wrench you out of misery and show you the glory of the world as if it were a brand-new discovery. You can start the day hopeless and end it knowing that everything is going to be OK. Life can change very, very quickly, often from a source that you never would have expected.

I love the sense in this poem of an unfurling of possibility and excitement. Suddenly happiness is not only plausible, but rushing out of you like a flock of birds in flight that bowl you over and leave you breathless and laughing. There is a sense of such joy, gratitude, and wonder in this poem that I challenge anyone to read it without experiencing at least an echo of that feeling in themselves.

I give this to patients to let them know that they have something to look forward to. One day soon the eyes of their eyes will be opened, and they will be able to see the world for what it is: glorious and infinite and yes. Soon, I tell them, this flood of happiness will be yours. And when it happens, you will suddenly know that it was always inevitable.

"I THANK YOU GOD"
e. e. cummings

i thank You God for most this amazing
day:for the leaping greenly spirits of trees
and a blue true dream of sky;and for everything
which is natural which is infinite which is yes

(i who have died am alive again today,
and this is the sun's birthday;this is the birth
day of life and love and wings:and of the gay
great happening illimitably earth)

how should tasting touching hearing seeing
breathing any—lifted from the no
of all nothing—human merely being
doubt unimaginable You?

(now the ears of my ears awake and
now the eyes of my eyes are opened)

Condition | Psychological Scarring

Also suitable for: EMOTIONAL BAGGAGE • FEELINGS OF
BROKENNESS • CYNICISM • FEAR OF VULNERABILITY •
SELF-ISOLATION

Most of us feel as though we are damaged in one way or another: that there is something within us that is broken beyond repair. Perhaps we only have a small crack. Perhaps there is a chasm within us. Either way, Izumi Shikibu's poem "Although the wind" wonderfully shows us that we should appreciate ourselves, flaws and all. Although we may find that our vulnerabilities, like a gap in the roof of a ruined house, leave us prone to being tossed about by the wind and the rain of an uncaring world, it might also be that without them we'd be missing out on a transcendent view of the moon. We run a risk when we allow ourselves to be moved, or to love, or to feel. We leave ourselves open to pain—a powerful disincentive. But could we imagine being moved by a work of art or a beautiful view if it didn't resonate with the "broken" part inside of us? There can be no beauty without the ghost of pain held within it.

Better than we do today, the ancients understood that darkness and light, love and pain, have always gone hand in hand. In the original Japanese, these lines are about a thousand years old, and yet they perfectly express the agony and the insight that come with being emotionally open. Of course, we could choose to patch over our cracks, to build up our walls and our roofs until the wind can't shake us. But would it be worth it, if in so doing we also shut out all chance of new feeling, new light? Sometimes, it is good to be shaken.

"ALTHOUGH THE WIND"
Izumi Shikibu, translated by Jane Hirshfield
with Mariko Aratani

Although the wind
blows terribly here,
the moonlight also leaks
between the roof planks
of this ruined house.

Condition | Existential Crisis

Also suitable for: MUNDANITY • BOREDOM

Sometimes you can get so caught up in the jumble of life, the pace and relentlessness of it, that you forget the fundamental amazement of it all. That there should be a world at all, particles and stars and gravity, is an inexplicable wonder. That we are present, too, not only here but conscious, experiencing joy and memory and all the thousands of things that we feel every day, is extraordinary beyond the mind's power to understand.

And it is our minds' limitations, I think, that tip us back into our mundane concerns and irritations. The sheer improbability of the world, its strangeness and its hugeness, is too much for us to consider for long. We are not equipped to understand the enormity of what we are and where we are, let alone why we are. Alongside the wonder and the gratitude, there is a terrible fear. Fear of the unknown is nothing next to fear of the unknowable.

Is it any wonder, then, that we retreat to our little internal courts, where petty problems vie for our attention, and diversions in their belled caps prance for our amusement? No. In the safety of our own little worlds, we can ignore the larger questions and the larger certainties. How much easier it is to fear an exam result than one's own insignificance in the overwhelming grandeur of the cosmos.

What this poem teaches us is that when the curtain falls back, and we are again presented with that terrifying mystery, we must learn to be brave. However uncomfortable it may be, it is only by confronting the primary wonder of the world that we can understand it in any depth. Denise Levertov shows us that if we are to truly inhabit the universe, we must look it in the eye with awe and gratitude. And then we must take what we have learned in that moment of understanding, and use it as perspective. Ultimately, to become humbled and small in the great cosmos is much more important than battling with the traffic warden.

PRIMARY WONDER
Denise Levertov

Days pass when I forget the mystery.
Problems insoluble and problems offering
their own ignored solutions
jostle for my attention, they crowd its antechamber
along with a host of diversions, my courtiers, wearing
their colored clothes; cap and bells.
                    And then
once more the quiet mystery
is present to me, the throng's clamor
recedes: the mystery
that there is anything, anything at all,
let alone cosmos, joy, memory, everything,
rather than void: and that, O Lord,
Creator, Hallowed One, you still,
hour by hour sustain it.

Condition | Old Age

Also suitable for: DESPAIR AT THE ABSURDITY OF THE WORLD •
EXISTENTIAL ANGST • HOPELESSNESS • PESSIMISM

When people tell me in the Pharmacy that their lives can't get better—that they've had their shot and now things are irredeemably bad—I often give them this poem. It appeals to the elderly, many of whom see their lives as winding down and getting progressively worse. I also offer it to those who are fragile, or who've suffered a loss from which they believe they will never recover—sometimes, for example, the death of a child.

All of these people have reason to be pessimistic. Their expectations of the world have been dashed, even if those expectations amount to little more than that inescapably naive, subconscious belief we all share: that aging and death will never actually happen to *us*. Yet there is also room for hope in even the most hopeless of existences. Into each life, some sun must fall.

There is a fairy-tale belief that we all hold on to, deep down, that things will be fair and that the things that happen, to us and to others, will basically make sense. When this expectation is frustrated, we lose our sense that the world has a narrative and a guiding principle. This can be desolating.

A poem like J. R. R. Tolkien's "All That Is Gold Does Not Glitter," with its almost Arthurian final couplet, offers back that faith in justice and goodness. It gives us hope that the right and the good can triumph in what seems a godless and random world: that there will be order again, and a framework through which we can understand our pain. The metaphor of life as a narrative comes up again and again in my Poetry Pharmacy precisely because it's so powerful—and Tolkien's poem emphatically drives it home. We just need to wait for the cycle to complete itself, it tells us. The worst thing we can do is stop reading before the end of the story.

ALL THAT IS GOLD DOES NOT GLITTER
J. R. R. Tolkien

All that is gold does not glitter,
Not all those who wander are lost;
The old that is strong does not wither,
Deep roots are not reached by the frost.

From the ashes a fire shall be woken,
A light from the shadows shall spring;
Renewed shall be blade that was broken,
The crownless again shall be king.

Condition | Glumness

Also suitable for: FEAR OF BEING UNLOVED • LOSS OF
PERSPECTIVE • WEARINESS • FEELINGS OF
UNATTRACTIVENESS

When we think about the things life still has in store, it can seem that our best days are behind us. We may be middle-aged and single, and fear we will never again be caught up in the whirlwind of infatuation. We may despair that we are unattractive, and will always remain so. Sometimes, we think we carry an incredibly heavy burden—only to realize that, as my late father would have said, "It's all in the mind."

When I talk to someone who seems to be struggling, but who I know would have the strength to shrug off all their burdens if only they could bring themselves to do so, I tend to show them Adrian Mitchell's brief poem "Celia Celia." There's a wonderful bathos to moving so swiftly from such deep and dreadful thoughts to an intensely simple solution. So you're sad. So you're hopeless. So what? There'll always be a naked Celia to picture, when High Holborn (a street in London) seems too depressing to be walked alone.

The poem isn't merely flippant. I also use it to comfort people, like the ones I mentioned above, who worry that the days of sex and flirtation have fled with their youth. Our society is fixated on the idea that only the smooth-faced, flexible young are entitled to these sorts of pleasures, but we should allow this poem to remind us that this is a terrible fallacy. There will always be someone who wants to liven up their commute with a mental image of us, wrinkled knees and all. The trick is simply to find them, and then to have the courage to show them what we've got.

CELIA CELIA
Adrian Mitchell

When I am sad and weary
When I think all hope has gone
When I walk along High Holborn
I think of you with nothing on

Condition | Purposelessness

Also suitable for: APATHY • NIHILISM

The implied question at the heart of William Stafford's poem "The Way It Is" is quite simple: "What is your thread?" Intuitively, when I first read it, I felt that I knew what mine was—and yet if you asked me to explain it, I would have nothing to say. It would be almost a parody of words to define it. Yet somehow the idea that I really am holding on to a thread reassures me, and affords a sense of stability through the upsets and dramas of everyday life.

For some, the thread may be spirituality; for others, fate, or love, or ambition. For others still, it may be something less grandiose: supporting friends, restoring old furniture, collecting every Smiths single ever released. Our threads are those fragile continuities of purpose, of passion, and of spirit that give us our sense of self and identity. And truly, the more we try to define what that thread of reassurance and possibility is, the more disservice we do to that feeling.

I do think, though, that there is a place for *hunting down* our threads when we fear we may have dropped them along the way. Some people come to my Poetry Pharmacy feeling completely lost—yet, if we piece together their story, we will often find a thread of some wonderment that they were unable to see clearly on their own, something that has become banal to them precisely because it is so fundamental.

In troubled times, our vision can become so blurred with anxiety (or quite literally blurred by tears) that we can't see what's in front of us. When people rediscover the thread that runs through their story, it is often a revelation. They are no longer directionless; suddenly, their narrative has the potential for a fitting ending—or for continuation down a previously unseen path.

THE WAY IT IS
William Stafford

There's a thread you follow. It goes among
things that change. But it doesn't change.
People wonder about what you are pursuing.
You have to explain about the thread.
But it is hard for others to see.
While you hold it you can't get lost.
Tragedies happen; people get hurt
or die; and you suffer and get old.
Nothing you do can stop time's unfolding.
You don't ever let go of the thread.

Condition | Unkindness to Oneself

Also suitable for: NEED FOR SELF-CARE • LETHARGY

If you could live your life over again, what would you do differently? What mistakes would you remedy, if you were given the chance? Perhaps you'd take a different career path, marry a different person, or skip that first marriage altogether. Perhaps you'd just launch yourself in an entirely different direction and hope things turned out better. Or perhaps, if you're anything like Raymond Carver, you'd look at your mistakes and recognize them for what they were: necessary hurdles that forced you to become the person you are.

In this poem Carver paints us a picture of self-acceptance that is simultaneously relatable and aspirational. We can all imagine wanting to stay in bed and read instead of facing a rainy day. But can we imagine how it would feel to give that morning to ourselves, as if it were a gift, and to accept it with no self-recrimination or guilt? Can we imagine lying in bed, remembering all the unforgivable things we've done, and pardoning ourselves for them?

What Carver alludes to, and what we would all do well to consider, is that it is only through our mistakes that we grow as human beings. How many of us have been given advice that seemed trite, only to discover the hard way that it was right all along? Ultimately, it is only through discovering life's painful lessons for ourselves that we can develop. Contentment is marvelous in the moment, but rather less useful in the long term.

The difficulty with learning from one's mistakes is that those lessons can often come hand in hand with regret and self-recrimination. Carver shows us another way. If we can manage to nurture ourselves, to forgive ourselves for those seemingly "unforgivable" and yet unavoidable mistakes, then we have the best of both worlds. Humans do dreadful things sometimes, when they're young, or scared, or stupid—but you don't need to be punished for being human. So stay in bed if you want to. Read a book, or just watch the drips run down the window. But whatever you do, remember to tell yourself it's OK. Tell yourself you'd do it all again, given half a chance.

RAIN
Raymond Carver

Woke up this morning with
a terrific urge to lie in bed all day
and read. Fought against it for a minute.

Then looked out the window at the rain.
And gave over. Put myself entirely
in the keep of this rainy morning.

Would I live my life over again?
Make the same unforgivable mistakes?
Yes, given half a chance. Yes.

Condition | Need for Reassurance

Also suitable for: ANXIETY • DEPRESSION • GENERAL FEAR • FEAR OF MORTALITY • PESSIMISM

There are moments in life when the banal suddenly, and quite without warning, becomes the transcendent. Perhaps a shaft of afternoon light paints a familiar view an unfamiliar gold; perhaps dust in a sunbeam or the dance of sparks above a fire transport you, for a long instant, to somewhere else altogether. The almost magical-seeming reflections of ripples on a ceiling are transfixing in just the same way.

In moments like these—awestruck moments when the ferocious beauty of the everyday catches us unawares—we are often moved to a reassessment. One flash of sunlight can be all it takes to give us the sense of possibility that can change everything. As a great sufferer from depression myself, I find a small moment like this, a sudden splash of serenity and beauty, can provide the impetus needed to turn my mood around. Not completely, perhaps, and not permanently—but sometimes a small push is all any of us is waiting for.

Derek Mahon's poem "Everything Is Going to Be All Right" describes wonderfully the feeling of that little push and reassessment. And there's something hugely powerful, too, about its final line. When my children are suffering and I hold them in my arms, it seems to be the most natural mantra in the world: *Everything will be all right*. There's a comfort to those words, whether or not they'll prove to be true. Of course, some wounds don't heal, and some wrongs go unrighted. But in the grander sense, in the *everything* sense, things do tend to be all right.

Too often, our pain is either in our heads or magnified beyond all proportion. If we can learn to manage it, if we can find that oasis of calm in the reflection of the waves, then we might find that our problems are not as all-consuming as we imagined. We might find that, in the end, everything really will be all right.

EVERYTHING IS GOING TO BE ALL RIGHT
Derek Mahon

How should I not be glad to contemplate
the clouds clearing beyond the dormer window
and a high tide reflected on the ceiling?
There will be dying, there will be dying,
but there is no need to go into that.
The poems flow from the hand unbidden
and the hidden source is the watchful heart.
The sun rises in spite of everything
and the far cities are beautiful and bright.
I lie here in a riot of sunlight
watching the day break and the clouds flying.
Everything is going to be all right.

Condition | Intractable Sorrow

Also suitable for: SADNESS • DEPRESSION • EMOTIONAL SCARRING

Who would have thought that a sorrow could be beautiful? And yet in Lucille Clifton's marvelous poem, we are offered a vision of sorrows circling us like moths entranced, loving us even as they torment us. They are not entirely of our world. They do not understand us, just as we do not understand them. And yet here they are, attaching themselves, staying faithfully by our sides, our companions throughout life.

Clifton compares sorrows to scars, and in some ways this seems a violent description. But what is a scar but a part of us that once was hurt, and is now stronger? Our scars are the record books of our lives, the risks we chose to take and the injuries we overcame. Perhaps our sorrows are something similar. Our sorrows bear important lessons, if only we can muster the courage to listen to them.

Pain is a very simple feeling, and yet it bears an extraordinary complexity as well. Maybe this is why it fuels our creativity so endlessly. But our pain can only be valuable to us if we are willing to examine it. It's only through getting to know our sorrows better that we can transmute their beauty into our own lives, whether that be through some artistic endeavor, or simply by coming to understand ourselves in greater depth.

Embracing our sorrows is also the only way of persuading them to unlatch that unwavering grip they have on us. So don't try to drown out their buzzing; don't try to bat them away. Welcome your sorrows, as you would a friend or a guest to your life. Let them perch on you for a while, like a particularly bold butterfly. And yet by the same token, don't clutch them to you. Don't enjoy their company too much. One day they're going to want to fly away; and you're going to have to let them.

SORROWS
Lucille Clifton

who would believe them winged
who would believe they could be

beautiful   who would believe
they could fall so in love with mortals

that they would attach themselves
as scars attach and ride the skin

sometimes we hear them in our dreams
rattling their skulls   clicking their bony fingers

envying our crackling hair
our spice filled flesh

they have heard me beseeching
as I whispered into my own

cupped hands   enough not me again
enough   but who can distinguish

one human voice
amid such choruses of desire

Condition | Hopelessness

Also suitable for: DESPAIR • LONELINESS • PESSIMISM

It's no surprise to me that fifty thousand fans of Liverpool Football Club sing the words of this song by Oscar Hammerstein before every match at Anfield. I suspect that if I told them afterward, "I love that poem you sang," they might not treat me with quite the same warmth; but it does, all the same, seem to me to work very well as just that—a poem on the page.

"You'll Never Walk Alone" is all about a seemingly simple concept: hope. Recently, politicians and talent-show hosts have appealed to hope rather liberally, to the extent that it's easy to assume the idea has been devalued. Yet hope is what keeps us going—it always has been.

Humans need more than food and shelter to survive: we also need a reason to keep going. We can find that in simple things like sugar or caffeine; but more important are our complex motivations, like friendship, hope, and the narratives in which we locate ourselves and our possibilities. Of those motivations, it is hope above all that can always, *always* be summoned. Even when all else has abandoned us, a sense of hope, of possibility, can be called up by nothing more than the will to look with quiet determination on the desolation around us.

The words of this particular poem inspire us to search for hope and to cling to it, so that we have solace in the loneliness and despair of the storm. So long as we have dreams of better times to keep us company, we are not alone. I advise learning it by heart if you can, and keeping it ready for when life becomes difficult. There's nothing like an inspiring anthem to get you through the wind and the rain.

from YOU'LL NEVER WALK ALONE

Oscar Hammerstein II

Walk on through the wind,
Walk on through the rain,
Tho' your dreams be tossed and blown.
Walk on, walk on, with hope in your heart
And you'll never walk alone.
You'll never walk alone.

Condition | Feelings of Unreality

Also suitable for: APATHY · BOREDOM · MESSINESS ·
PURPOSELESSNESS · NEED FOR SELF-CARE

Many years ago, I read an extraordinary book in which a woman visits one of the wisest men in India. He tells her that an important reason we in the modern world have lost our sense of reality, of connection with life, is that we have lost the inclination to do menial tasks for ourselves: to wash our own laundry, to clean our own plates, to prepare food properly. These daily tasks, he tells her, are what give us purpose and meaning. When his young visitor asks, "But how can I go out and help the world?" he responds, "How can you help others when you don't even know how to help yourself?"

There's something essential and joyful about our domestic duties: they have a meditative quality that gives us space to think lightly, without direction or the need to be immediately useful. Sometimes we need to turn our day-to-day brains off in order to connect with something deeper. It's no coincidence that most of us think of our best ideas when we're not trying.

In the long run, menial tasks are also a great cure for directionlessness. There is a lot to be said for what people today call "self-care": doing things with the express intent of making yourself feel cared for. You may not know where your life is going, but you certainly know what will happen if you don't do your laundry or don't wash your hair. In their mundanity and repetitiveness, these tasks give you a rhythm, which in turn becomes a kind of structure, which, ultimately, will give you the ability to cope.

With these tasks, some of the oppressive weight of choice is lifted: they are always there, always suggesting themselves. However lost you feel, try to carve out time to make your bed. In doing something so simple, you actually begin to learn how to untangle the complexities of life.

from OF GRAVITY AND LIGHT
John Burnside

What we need most, we learn from the menial tasks:
the novice raking sand in Buddhist texts,
or sweeping leaves, his hands chilled to the bone,
while understanding hovers out of reach;
the changeling in a folk tale, chopping logs,
poised at the dizzy edge of transformation;

and everything they do is gravity:
swaying above the darkness of the well
to haul the bucket in; guiding the broom;
finding the body's kinship with the earth
beneath their feet, the lattice of a world
where nothing turns or stands outside the whole;

and when the insight comes, they carry on
with what's at hand: the gravel path; the fire;
knowing the soul is no more difficult
than water, or the fig tree by the well
that stood for decades, barren and inert,
till every branch was answered in the stars.

Condition | Emotional Baggage

Also suitable for: PSYCHOLOGICAL SCARRING • TRAUMA •
TRUST ISSUES

There's something very important about the realization that our sorrows are separate from us. Our experiences shape us, of course, and our pain helps to mold us: the things we have known and felt weigh heavy on our thinking when we ask ourselves who, and how, we would like to be. But it is we who choose how to respond to our pain, how to shore ourselves up against it, and, ultimately, whether to continue carrying it at all.

When you feel weighed down by your past, it is all too easy to assume that it must have become an integral part of you, one that you will never shrug off. But just as the mule in Jane Hirshfield's poem "Burlap Sack" is not its load, your self is not the experiences it has gathered. Think how different the world would seem if, like that mule, you could let go of that incredible weight and let your ears waggle like a happy dog's tail.

Of course, transformation is never as easy as taking off a pack or dropping a weight. Letting go of the past takes work, and it may be a process that takes a lifetime. But knowing that it's possible, that you are not indelibly marked by your sorrows and your grief, is what is crucial. Acknowledging the possibility of change or evolution is the first step toward achieving it. In the end, you are not your sorrows. However hard it seems, try to entertain the possibility that you might be a happy mule suffering a temporary inconvenience. Allow yourself to believe it can be overcome.

BURLAP SACK
Jane Hirshfield

A person is full of sorrow
the way a burlap sack is full of stones or sand.
We say, "Hand me the sack,"
but we get the weight.
Heavier if left out in the rain.
To think that the sand or stones are the self is an error.
To think that grief is the self is an error.
Self carries grief as a pack mule carries the side bags,
being careful between the trees to leave extra room.
The mule is not the load of ropes and nails and axes.
The self is not the miner nor builder nor driver.
What would it be to take the bride
and leave behind the heavy dowry?
To let the thin-ribbed mule browse the tall grasses,
its long ears waggling like the tails of two happy dogs?

Condition | Convalescence

There is a sameness about serious illness: that forced withdrawal from the world of the everyday into a sort of twilit existence. Often, those who are confronted with this other world for the first time are dismayed by it, by the solitude and triviality of life as an invalid. But Julia Darling shows us something more. In her poem "Chemotherapy," we see a life that has been made small, but which cannot be made inconsequential.

This is a poem that all the sick, regardless of their illness, might find comfort in reading—but its explicit subject is, of course, cancer. Cancer is in everybody's lives these days; few of us have not been touched by it, at least tangentially. Indeed, the healthier we become as a society, the more cancer threatens us: after all, if nothing else gets us, then we can be pretty sure that cancer will in the end. The particular horror of cancer, though, is chemotherapy, that seemingly contradictory method by which we poison the sick faster than the cancer ever could. It's always a shock for anyone to experience chemo, or to care about someone who does.

Small pleasures, savored intently, can bring pleasure to the darkest times. The taste of tea hot on the tongue, the softness of a shawl—it is truly wondrous that such simple matters can be life enhancing, and yet somehow they are. If only we could all remain aware, when we are bustling and fretting through our normal lives, that the smallest, quietest things are gifts.

CHEMOTHERAPY
Julia Darling

I did not imagine being bald
at forty four. I didn't have a plan.
Perhaps a scar or two from growing old,
hot flushes. I'd sit fluttering a fan.

But I am bald, and hardly ever walk
by day, I'm the invalid of these rooms,
stirring soups, awake in the half dark,
not answering the phone when it rings.

I never thought that life could get this small,
that I would care so much about a cup,
the taste of tea, the texture of a shawl,
and whether or not I should get up.

I'm not unhappy. I have learnt to drift
and sip. The smallest things are gifts.

Condition | Loneliness

Also suitable for: GENERAL MALAISE • LOSS OF MOTIVATION • LACK OF SELF-BELIEF • LOW SELF-ESTEEM • LACK OF SUPPORT

Loneliness is among the most common conditions of the modern age, much exacerbated by the constant presence of social media feeds filled with jokes you don't get, parties you haven't been invited to, and friends you don't have. Even if you've been with a different friend every night for a week, the feed can reduce you to rubble the moment it gets you alone again.

To protect ourselves from being found out as the flawed, occasionally unsociable beings we are, we conjure avatars of ourselves that project nothing but success, happiness, and well-being. Yet, in a very human way, we find it impossible to see others' avatars for what they are. In our minds, *we* are the only fakers. For anyone who is lonely or miserable, this trickle of envy produces a slow erosion of self-esteem. And, as everyone knows, slow erosion—given time—can create a chasm.

Poets have been describing the malaise of the way we live now—the dehumanizing isolation of city living, the sense of being one identical face among many—for centuries. Yet somehow it still seems modern, confusing, an unexpected slap from a supposedly benign world. Knowing that, paradoxically, we are not alone in our loneliness can be a revelation.

When this issue comes up in the Pharmacy, I read and give my patients a copy of these four extraordinary and inspiring lines by Hafiz, now around seven hundred years old. I encourage them to learn the poem by heart, and to stick it on their mirror so that they will read it every morning. Some time ago I received a message from a patient, telling me how she had returned to her apartment to find it ransacked by burglars. The only thing that hadn't been disturbed was the Hafiz poem stuck on her mirror. "Thank you," she wrote. "It got me through the night."

Motivations

Condition | Inertia When Alone

Also suitable for: FEELINGS OF INADEQUACY • INSECURITY •
NEED FOR SELF-CARE • SELF-RECRIMINATION

I see a lot of people in my Pharmacy sessions who tell me that they can't do anything when they're on their own. If they had a visitor, they could entertain: cook, buy food, be cheerful and welcoming. Yet somehow the motivation to do this for themselves is very hard to come by. Left alone, they don't believe that they're worth the effort. Similarly, I meet person after person who funnels all their energy into helping and caring for others, yet has no regard for their own well-being. It's as if they see themselves as the only people on earth not deserving of love and kindness. There's a fundamental unfairness in this: a sense that people are willfully selling themselves short.

It seems to me that a crucial objective of existence is to come to terms with oneself. Learning to like ourselves is something we all battle with, young and old. It's a constant, permanent progression, and it's never truly complete. But when you can look yourself in the eye and actually cherish yourself—when you can recognize who you are with all your faults, and be happy with that—then you'll see that you are no less worthy of kindness than your friends and guests. You'll be able to speak kindly and politely to yourself, no longer tearing yourself down as you might an enemy, but instead bolstering and encouraging yourself as you would anyone else.

We devote so much time to self-analysis in our modern lives, to wondering why we aren't happy or whether other people see our flaws as plainly as we do. Many of us resort to pills and alcohol, and sometimes even less healthy habits, just to keep ourselves in some semblance of balance. Yet all most of us really need is to come to terms with who we are. Unfortunately, there is not an over-the-counter remedy for this. Fortunately, however, it is entirely within our grasp.

LOVE AFTER LOVE
Derek Walcott

The time will come
when, with elation,
you will greet yourself arriving
at your own door, in your own mirror,
and each will smile at the other's welcome,

and say, sit here. Eat.
You will love again the stranger who was your self.
Give wine. Give bread. Give back your heart
to itself, to the stranger who has loved you

all your life, whom you ignored
for another, who knows you by heart.
Take down the love-letters from the bookshelf,

the photographs, the desperate notes,
peel your own image from the mirror.
Sit. Feast on your life.

Condition | Stagnation

Also suitable for: APATHY • DEPRESSION • DESPAIR • GRIEF

It's easy to forget sometimes that however old we are, we still have the capacity to grow. This poem is a reminder that it's never too late to bud, bloom, and flourish; that winter only lasts as long as we allow it to. Philip Larkin expresses the wonder of that extraordinary potential for change. It's the feeling we recognize in the seemingly barren bush as it edges its way toward budding. We know, intuitively and intensely, that transformation is on its way. In a matter of weeks, that bush will be all but unrecognizable. It will be fully alive again.

Have you ever had a thought on your lips—an "I love you," or even a simple "yes"—and sensed the huge power the next moment will have over your life? This, suggests Larkin, is your own bud, the leaf about to spring forth from you and into life. This moment before speaking, when we stand poised on the edge of transforming our world in some huge, almost unthinkable manner—though we may not always feel it, this is a power we all possess within us, every second of every day.

Our minds are amazing, quick-blooming things. We have the ability, if we believe it enough, to give ourselves a push that will eventually spill us out of any period of stagnation, grief, or depression. One day we may notice the tiniest of buds at the tip of one of our frostbitten branches; and before we know it, we will be green and vibrant once more.

Should we resent the trees their ability to bud anew, asks Larkin? No—they die just like we do. We are all heading to the same place. Yet within our allotted span, growing in us like the rings of a tree, we have lifetime after lifetime. We will always have that chance to be reborn into positivity and change. Grab it. Begin afresh, afresh, afresh.

THE TREES
Philip Larkin

The trees are coming into leaf
Like something almost being said;
The recent buds relax and spread,
Their greenness is a kind of grief.

Is it that they are born again
And we grow old? No, they die too,
Their yearly trick of looking new
Is written down in rings of grain.

Yet still the unresting castles thresh
In fullgrown thickness every May.
Last year is dead, they seem to say,
Begin afresh, afresh, afresh.

Condition ⦙ Lack of Courage

Also suitable for: FEAR • LACK OF CONFIDENCE •
LACK OF CONVICTION

Taking a risk can be a terrifying thing—and I say that as some-
one who has started more ventures than I can count. Every
one of us has known the peculiar vulnerability of putting not only
our physical assets and safety but also our own ego on the line
when taking a leap of faith. What is remarkable is how much
harder it is to take that step than it is to pick ourselves up again if it
fails. If only we had the courage of our convictions and were willing
to fail every now and again, we would achieve so much more.

Many patients in my Poetry Pharmacy tell me that they feel
they lack the requisite courage to make the leap in life that they
have always dreamed of, whether it might be to write, paint, end
a relationship, start a relationship, or simply confront something
that has frightened them.

People can spend entire lifetimes putting off the risks that
might make them the happiest. I can't tell you the number of peo-
ple I've met who've spent thirty years, sometimes even longer,
dreaming of changing their lives and never daring. It leads to a
sort of paralysis of the soul, which undercuts all of life's pleasures
and stops you from evolving. When fear keeps you from pursuing
your goals, it's like you've stopped writing the story of your exis-
tence halfway through. And no one wants to look back upon their
life as a potential masterpiece that never quite made it.

I often prescribe this poem to people who have lost their confi-
dence and, like the Cowardly Lion in *The Wizard of Oz*, are in need
of encouragement. It shows how a leap into the unknown—
whether it's a bungee jump or a marriage proposal—can lead to
joy, not disaster.

COME TO THE EDGE

Christopher Logue

Come to the edge.
We might fall.
Come to the edge.
It's too high!
COME TO THE EDGE!
And they came,
And he pushed,
And they flew.

Condition ¦ Pessimism

Also suitable for: LOVE OF MISERY • GLOOMINESS

This is a wonderful poem for bringing perspective to even the most intractable-seeming problem. Ha Jin shows us that however bleak we may believe our lives to be, and however loud our whining, things could always be worse. How can we tell that they could be? Because we are not yet laughing.

There is a point where misery, through sheer persistence, becomes humor. Tragedy plus time equals comedy, we are told, and yet somehow we forget that when tragedy is protracted it has enough time to ferment into comedy all by itself. Sometimes the only way to cope with life and its deprivations is to laugh in its face. After all, for many this is the only defiance left to them.

What's particularly interesting about this poem is the recognition it offers, in the first stanza, of the desirability of misery. When we are short on things to complain about, it is always tempting to find something extra to add to our bank of grievances. After all, sorrow adds spice to life; it gives us something to think and emote about when everything else is flat and dull. And yet, ask anyone who has been through real trauma—displacement, bereavement, any true loss—and they will tell you that they wish they'd appreciated the good times more.

There is a charm to a distressed face, just as there is a charm to being able to feel poetic distress about one's own life. And yet that charm only lives as long as our naivete; it only lasts until we lose something we can hardly bear to live without. But even then, this poem offers us comfort. You may lose everything, it tells us, but you will never lose your sense of humor, or of what is beautiful. Even sorrow, even the destruction of strawberries in the fields, can be beautiful. There is still time to laugh, and to wonder at the world around you. Nothing can take that away.

WAYS OF TALKING
Ha Jin

We used to like talking about grief
Our journals and letters were packed
with losses, complaints, and sorrows.
Even if there was no grief
we wouldn't stop lamenting
as though longing for the charm
of a distressed face.

Then we couldn't help expressing grief
So many things descended without warning:
labor wasted, loves lost, houses gone,
marriages broken, friends estranged,
ambitions worn away by immediate needs.
Words lined up in our throats
for a good whining.
Grief seemed like an endless river—
the only immortal flow of life.

After losing a land and then giving up a tongue,
we stopped talking of grief
Smiles began to brighten our faces.
We laugh a lot, at our own mess.
Things become beautiful,
even hailstones in the strawberry fields.

Condition ┊ Defeatism

Also suitable for: APATHY • DISCOURAGEMENT • PESSIMISM • LACK OF SELF-BELIEF • LOW SELF-ESTEEM

In my own life, I'm very familiar with the difference self-belief can make to performance. When I'm feeling a bit flat and useless, I can see the difference spelled out in the way I engage with the world and those around me. I cannot inspire excitement and confidence in others because I have lost them in myself. Perhaps I should have Walter D. Wintle's poem "Thinking" taped to the inside of my jacket as a crib sheet.

So many people come to my Pharmacy and say, "I think I'm beaten. I'm destroyed." This is always heartbreaking to hear; but if I think they have enough emotional and physical strength to turn it around, then I don't treat them gently. Instead, I give them this poem as a sort of kick in the pants. If you walk in and say, "I'm going to lose," before you've even tried, you haven't got a chance.

Sometimes, the only way is to talk yourself into it—whatever "it" may be. Although it is useful for all ages, I find myself prescribing this poem particularly frequently to young people and teenagers: people who are just getting started in life, and who may have taken a few knocks on the way, but who really only need a supportive sense of self-belief to get going. As your parents probably told you: whatever you want to do, you can achieve it with hard work and self-belief. Or, at least, without those things, you'll never achieve anything worth having.

THINKING
Walter D. Wintle

If you think you are beaten, you are;
    If you think you dare not, you don't.
If you'd like to win, but think you can't,
    It's almost a cinch you won't.

If you think you'll lose, you're lost,
    For out of the world we find
Success begins with a fellow's will,
    It's all in the state of mind.

If you think you're outclassed, you are;
    You've got to think high to rise;
You've got to be sure of yourself before
    You can ever win a prize.

Life's battles don't always go
    To the stronger or faster man;
But soon or late the man who wins,
    Is the one who *thinks he can*.

Condition | Dissatisfaction with Life

Also suitable for: EXISTENTIAL ANGST • FAILURE • LACK OF JOB
FULFILLMENT • FALLING OUT OF LOVE • WASTED POTENTIAL

How many of us can say with absolute sincerity that we haven't felt dissatisfied with our lives and our achievements from time to time? That we haven't been swept away, all of a sudden, by a sense of what we could have been, and are not?

Nobody achieves everything that, in the optimism of youth, they once believed they would. Often, even the young are dissatisfied with what they've done in their short time. We might never have the lives we see in magazines, with the perfect kitchen and immaculate jaw-dropper of a spouse. And yet the open secret, the secret we all conveniently forget as soon as it becomes time to start pitying ourselves, is that the people in the magazines don't either—because in real life, nothing is perfect. People get messy, and things go missing.

But my purpose here is not to tell you that your life is actually the best you can hope for. No, the way this poem will improve things is by encouraging you to evaluate your life sensibly: to ask yourself how far your life reflects your own priorities and choices, and whether they have ultimately been the right ones for you. It might also prompt you to reflect on how lucky you have been compared to others—as well as on how you could help to alleviate the burdens of those around you.

Are you idly wistful for another life, as every other member of our perennially dissatisfied species is? Are there ambitions you gave up on long ago that still haunt you? Is there a lost love out there who might be pining right back at you? If you look yourself in the eye, look that alternative life square on, and truly think you could be happier, you need to listen to that impulse. Remember that it's never too late to change things. It's never too late to be bold.

THE PRICE
Stuart Henson

Sometimes it catches when the fumes rise up
among the throbbing lights of cars, or as
you look away to dodge eye-contact with
your own reflection in the carriage-glass;
or in a waiting-room a face reminds you
that the colour supplements have lied
and some have pleasure and some pay the price.
Then all the small securities you built
about your house, your desk, your calendar
are blown like straws; and momentarily,
as if a scent of ivy or the earth
had opened up a childhood door, you pause,
to take the measure of what might have been
against the kind of life you settled for.

Condition | Procrastination

Also suitable for: APATHY • AMBITIONS UNREALIZED

Getting started. It's not easy, is it? If, like most of us, you are prone to procrastination, it can be easy to assume that there will come a better time to start. A time when the stars are aligned, when your ideas are better thought out, when you feel absolutely ready.

But here's the secret: nobody ever feels truly ready to start. Not if the enterprise is worth starting, anyway. Anything risky, or grand, or exciting, will always frighten us. We will never be totally poised to make the leap. And yet what this poem tells us so wonderfully is that this fact shouldn't hold us back. Waiting for the perfect moment, for time to have brought us the right thoughts and fate to have brought us the right gifts, will leave us waiting forever.

All we need, William Stafford tells us, is this moment: the moment when we decide to begin. When we carry our ambitions through the day and into evening, taking the first steps that will eventually be the foundation of miles run. All it takes is an effort of will, and of self-belief, to set us on the path to whatever it is we are so afraid to achieve.

It could be this moment, right now, that you look back upon as the beginning of it all. Imagine that. Imagine looking back on this moment and remembering, not the light through the window or the sounds of the street, but the very first clenching of resolve. The moment you turned around and actually did it—whatever it may be. Wouldn't that be something worth remembering?

YOU READING THIS, BE READY
William Stafford

Starting here, what do you want to remember?
How sunlight creeps along a shining floor?
What scent of old wood hovers, what softened
sound from outside fills the air?

Will you ever bring a better gift for the world
than the breathing respect that you carry
wherever you go right now? Are you waiting
for time to show you some better thoughts?

When you turn around, starting here, lift this
new glimpse that you found; carry into evening
all that you want from this day. This interval you spent
reading or hearing this, keep it for life—

What can anyone give you greater than now,
starting here, right in this room, when you turn around?

Condition | Need for Mindfulness

Also suitable for: DISCONNECTEDNESS • NEED FOR GRATITUDE

Prayer, to many in our secular age, has become a dirty word. The concept is dismissed as fusty or naive; the practice even more so. And yet, as the popularity of meditation and mindfulness soar, there seems to be a collective longing for a moment of quiet in our busy lives. A moment in which another voice—an internal whisper, all too easily drowned out behind the sirens and chatter of modern life—may speak.

Mark Oakley, a canon at St. Paul's Cathedral in London, wrote a wonderful book about how to him, liturgy was poetry. No matter the religion, he says, the devotional words we chant or memorize or sing are a kind of poetry that links us to the divine. In the case of many religions, those words can be in a language that the worshippers themselves don't even understand; and yet somehow the cadence of those words is enough to transport us.

It's not only the religious who can gain from prayer, just as it's not only the religious who can appreciate a spectacular cathedral, or mosque, or temple. Prayer is a constant that runs through all human civilizations, and it's there for a reason. Mary Oliver reminds us that we are all in need of a doorway into thanks; a way of relating to the world without our egos and, for just a moment, allowing ourselves to feel quiet gratitude for all the small moments of grace that we encounter daily. To thank the world around us for containing blue irises, and weeds, and small stones.

Stop in the street, in the garden, on the train. Pay attention. Put together a few simple words that feel right. If you're very quiet, and very lucky, you might just hear a voice whispering back to you.

PRAYING
Mary Oliver

It doesn't have to be
the blue iris, it could be
weeds in a vacant lot, or a few
small stones; just
pay attention, then patch

a few words together and don't try
to make them elaborate, this isn't
a contest but the doorway

into thanks, and a silence in which
another voice may speak.

Condition | **Lethargy**

Also suitable for: APATHY • DEPRESSION • LOSS OF PLEASURE
IN LIFE • SELF-ISOLATION • SELF-SABOTAGE

Many of us know the feeling of having sabotaged ourselves through inaction, whether for an hour, a day, a week, or even longer. Those of us who have struggled with depression recognize it particularly well: there is a breed of self-spiting apathy that can take hold of us and prevent us from even *wanting* to be happy. Often the things that will make us feel better—getting dressed, getting out into nature, taking joy in the small pleasures of life—are exactly the things we deny ourselves when we are at our lowest points. It's almost as if we were punishing ourselves for being sad.

However reluctantly, it is hugely important at these times that we seek out some simple, joyful activity—and there are very few pleasures so pure as leaving the first footprints in an expanse of untrodden snow. It's almost impossible to resist, when you get the chance. This is what makes the image at the end of Michael Laskey's poem "Nobody" so affecting: there is such poignant regret, such self-recrimination, as the poet closes those curtains. He has somehow let himself down. He has failed to appreciate the world as he should have done; and as he accepts his mistake, he swears he will never let it happen again.

If you don't do it, if you don't get out there and make an effort to have fun and to appreciate life, then you'll end the day feeling even worse for your lack of willpower. Remember: every moment is an opportunity to make a change. Give yourself permission to be happy, to be enthusiastic and undignified and carefree. If you pass up the chance, you'll never know what you've missed.

NOBODY
Michael Laskey

If you can't bring yourself to build
a snowman or even to clench
a snowball or two to fling
at the pine tree trunk, at least
find some reason to take you out

of yourself: scrape a patch of grass clear
for the birds maybe; prod at your shrubs
so they shake off the weight, straighten up;
or just stump about leaving prints
of your boots, your breath steaming out.

Promise. Don't let yourself in
for this moment again: the end
of the afternoon, drawing the curtains
on the glare of the garden, a whole
day of snow nobody's trodden.

Condition | Feelings of Worthlessness

Also suitable for: HOPELESSNESS • INERTIA • POINTLESSNESS • SELF-PITY

Sometimes, patients come to me at the Pharmacy with a feeling that nothing is worthwhile; that even trying to make things better is a waste of time. Their lives aren't a disaster; often they've got everything going for them. They may have interesting jobs, loving families, and active social lives, and yet these have somehow lost their luster. On the surface, these people acknowledge, their lives are good—even enviable. But this doesn't make it easier for them to break the cycle of self-pity that is holding them back.

When trying to make yourself happy doesn't work, and finding meaning in an outwardly meaningful life proves impossible, it's time for a change in perspective. Obviously, improving your own life in these circumstances won't alter how you feel. Instead, you should reach for the thing that reliably makes us all feel better about ourselves, trite as it may sound: improving others' lives. As Ella Wheeler Wilcox's poem "At Set of Sun" makes clear, it can be a completely effortless thing—all it takes is letting someone through a door ahead of you; a casual "I like your dress," or "You're very good at that." When you make someone else's day worthwhile, the poem reminds us, you're doing the same for your own.

This outlook takes you away from your own burdens and allows you to focus on someone else instead. There's no better way to break a cycle of self-pity, to find a sense of purpose and self-respect, or just to take your mind off your own misery. Attending to others puts you back in touch with the lives around you, helping you understand where you fit and how lucky you really are. You're lucky not just because you have much to be grateful for, but also because you have much to offer others.

from AT SET OF SUN
Ella Wheeler Wilcox

If we sit down at set of sun,
And count the things that we have done,
 And, counting, find
One self-denying act, one word
That eased the heart of him who heard,
 One glance, most kind,
That fell like sunshine where it went,
Then we may count that day well spent.

But if, through all the life-long day,
We've eased no heart by yea or nay;
 If through it all
We've done no thing that we can trace,
That brought the sunshine to a face,
 No act most small
That helped some soul, and nothing cost,
Then count that day as worse than lost.

Condition | Loss of Creativity

Also suitable for: REDISCOVERING INNER CHILD • INSPIRATION

There is a certain superpower that we all possessed, once upon a time. We see it still, outside the school gates, in playgrounds, smearing crayons along our walls. And yet, however much we may envy children's exuberance and vividity of imagination—for that, of course, is the superpower I mean—most of us feel we will never again recapture it.

But there is still much to be learned from children, and a great deal of that superpower that can be recouped by even the oldest and most hardened among us. All it takes is an overcoming of self-consciousness. Whatever a child may be imagining, they are always imagining it completely, with their whole self. There is no space left over for the nagging voice we adults will all recognize: the one that tells us that we are being judged, that we are ridiculous.

That essential freedom that is so central to true creativity—the freedom from the limiting parts of oneself—can feel impossible to some of my patients. They feel that as the scars and worries of their lives have accrued, they have become more limited. They will never again be able to live an unconstrained life, one without that collection of cruel voices in the back of their head.

I tell these patients not to despair. Recapturing that element of childishness is not easy, but it is far from impossible. Challenge yourself. Embarrass yourself. You don't need threads of silver or gold to create something of beauty. You don't need instruments. All you need is to remember how to be fully yourself.

THE ART ROOM
Shara McCallum

for my sisters

Because we did not have threads
of turquoise, silver, and gold,
we could not sew a sun nor sky.
And our hands became balls of fire.
And our arms spread open like wings.

Because we had no chalk or pastels,
no toad, forest, or morning-grass slats
of paper, we had no colour
for creatures. So we squatted
and sprang, squatted and sprang.

Four young girls, plaits heavy
on our backs, our feet were beating
drums, drawing rhythms from the floor;
our mouths became woodwinds;
our tongues touched teeth and were reeds.

Condition | Loss of Zest for Life

Also suitable for: LOSS OF MOTIVATION • LOSS OF PASSION •
NEED FOR SELF-CARE

It's the story of so many of our lives: we begin with a great enthu-
siasm, a great passion, but all too often we end up giving up on
it and the world for one reason or another. Maybe we've been dis-
appointed by ourselves, or by those around us. Maybe we've lost
our self-belief. No matter the reason, there's something deeply
dispiriting about losing whatever it was that used to animate us.

In Vicki Feaver's poem "Ironing," that passion isn't something
grand and overbearing. Instead, it's a simple task that—like it or
not—we have all had to perform at some point. It shows us that
the things that bring us pleasure in life, that motivate us to get out
of bed, don't have to be huge at all. Often, when something goes
wrong, it is the small acts of self-care that we abandon first—even
when they are the very things that have the power to heal us.

The speaker in the poem rediscovers her passion, and she finds
that it is as strong as ever. Through the ironing we see her life gain-
ing purpose, becoming joyful again where before it was crumpled
and unexciting. She has reclaimed her life along with her iron-
ing, and that passion has nosed its way into every corner, until
by the end we see her ironing her blouse into an airy shape with
room for her own body, her own heart: her life is molded to fit her
again, and there is room to breathe.

Whatever passion you have left behind you in life, whatever
hobbies or activities have given you joy and meaning, pick them
up again, and make your life one that fits you.

IRONING
Vicki Feaver

I used to iron everything:
my iron flying over sheets and towels
like a sledge chased by wolves over snow;

the flex twisting and crinking
until the sheath frayed, exposing
wires like nerves. I stood like a horse

with a smoking hoof,
inviting anyone who dared
to lie on my silver padded board,

to be pressed to the thinness
of dolls cut from paper.
I'd have commandeered a crane

if I could, got the welders at Jarrow
to heat me an iron the size of a tug
to flatten the house.

Then for years I ironed nothing.
I put the iron in a high cupboard.
I converted to crumpledness.

And now I iron again: shaking
dark spots of water onto wrinkled
silk, nosing into sleeves, round

continued . . .

buttons, breathing the sweet heated smell
hot metal draws from newly-washed
cloth, until my blouse dries

to a shining, creaseless blue,
an airy shape with room to push
my arms, breasts, lungs, heart into.

Condition | Failure to Live in the Moment

Also suitable for: FRETFULNESS • REGRET • SELF-RECRIMINATION • WORRYING

We've all been told to live in the moment before—it's become something of a catchphrase of self-help culture. But, just as with so many other seemingly simple pieces of advice, it can be very hard to know what "living in the moment" actually means, and what it might look like.

Buddhists sometimes talk about the "second arrow": the suffering we inflict on ourselves by worrying about future pain, or by regretting past mistakes. Sometimes, the things we dread surprise us by being far less awful than we feared; sometimes, our agony over a past deed is out of all proportion to the act itself. In such cases, it may be our thoughts, and not the reasons for them, that do the most damage: the second arrow is deadlier than the first. Evidently, we need to learn to avoid shooting that second arrow at all.

This, Mark Doty tells us, is where the golden retrievers come in. Ball, squirrel, pond—these are the ways that dogs navigate the world. Their day-to-day experience is exactly that: experience. If we could let the average well-looked-after dog teach us how to live as it does, to bounce from excitement to excitement without ever pausing for analysis, perhaps we could be as joyful as it is.

Tomorrow—if that's what you call it—can wait until tomorrow. Granted, living like a dog full time might not exactly be convenient—but for a few minutes? For the length of a walk? Surely we can respond to the rallying call, the Zen bow-wow of the golden retriever, for that long at least.

GOLDEN RETRIEVALS
Mark Doty

Fetch? Balls and sticks capture my attention
seconds at a time. Catch? I don't think so.
Bunny, tumbling leaf, a squirrel who's—oh
joy—actually scared. Sniff the wind, then

I'm off again: muck, pond, ditch, residue
of any thrillingly dead thing. And you?
Either you're sunk in the past, half our walk,
thinking of what you never can bring back,

or else you're off in some fog concerning
—tomorrow, is that what you call it? My work:
to unsnare time's warp (and woof!), retrieving,
my haze-headed friend, you. This shining bark,

a Zen master's bronzy gong, calls you here,
entirely, now: bow-wow, bow-wow, bow-wow.

Condition | Need for Moral Guidance

Also suitable for: AMBITIOUSNESS • ARROGANCE • FAILURE •
LACK OF SELF-BELIEF • LOSS OF SENSE OF SELF

If—" by Rudyard Kipling, is the UK's favorite poem by pretty much any metric. It wins every poll, and—what's more—a couplet from the poem is inscribed above the players' entrance to Wimbledon's Centre Court. You don't get any more British than that. Whenever I've read poems to people, particularly my children, this is the one that they've asked to hear again. This is the one that's inspired them most.

"If—" encodes a lot of what, at least according to British folklore, makes up our national identity. And yet it's about so much more than just "Britishness"—there's a nobility and a fortitude to the character Rudyard Kipling sketches here that can resonate with anyone, of any culture. Someone who is self-effacing, kind, thoughtful, brave, spirited, productive, and ultimately true to himself or (despite the of-its-time final line) *her*self.

The person Kipling describes is accessible and generous, and yet in some deeply personal way they are untouchable. Triumph and disaster, kings and crowds, can all distort the way we see ourselves, but none of them is under our control: Kipling's figure looks on them all with equanimity. We must remember that our successes and the esteem of others do not change who we are at our core—and should lead us neither into arrogance nor into self-doubt.

Kipling advises us to hold true to who we are, even in the face of corrupting influences. He reminds us that we have whole worlds within ourselves, and that we alone are the master of them. No outside influence, no person or circumstance, can touch these interior worlds without our permission. Neither foes nor loving friends can hurt us if we have a strong enough sense of self. That's a great lesson for all of us.

IF—
Rudyard Kipling

If you can keep your head when all about you
Are losing theirs and blaming it on you;
If you can trust yourself when all men doubt you,
But make allowance for their doubting too;
If you can wait and not be tired by waiting,
Or being lied about, don't deal in lies,
Or being hated, don't give way to hating,
And yet don't look too good, nor talk too wise;

If you can dream—and not make dreams your master;
If you can think—and not make thoughts your aim,
If you can meet with Triumph and Disaster
And treat those two impostors just the same;
If you can bear to hear the truth you've spoken
Twisted by knaves to make a trap for fools,
Or watch the things you gave your life to, broken,
And stoop and build 'em up with worn-out tools;

If you can make one heap of all your winnings
And risk it on one turn of pitch-and-toss,
And lose, and start again at your beginnings
And never breathe a word about your loss;
If you can force your heart and nerve and sinew
To serve your turn long after they are gone,
And so hold on when there is nothing in you
Except the Will which says to them: "Hold on!"

continued . . .

If you can talk with crowds and keep your virtue,
Or walk with Kings—nor lose the common touch,
If neither foes nor loving friends can hurt you,
If all men count with you, but none too much;
If you can fill the unforgiving minute
With sixty seconds' worth of distance run,
Yours is the Earth and everything that's in it,
And—which is more—you'll be a Man, my son!

Condition : Fear of Mortality

Also suitable for: PURPOSELESSNESS • GENERAL MALAISE

Most of us imagine that our final thought on our deathbeds will be, to some extent, about what we've achieved. What impact have we made on the world; who will remember us, and why? What have we achieved, and was it enough? In this poem Mary Oliver offers us another option. Perhaps it's not what we do, but how we live, that matters.

This poem reminds me of an event I attended many years ago, at a time before Buddhism was as popular as it is today. One of the Dalai Lama's inner circle was giving a talk to a rather hostile hall of people in Central London. At the end, a man put his hand up and rather pompously said, "Could you please tell me, in simple terms, the essential differences between your world and ours?"

"Well," said the monk, "when I was young the Dalai Lama sent me to Cambridge to study. And when I left, he told me to work in an English hospice, where I've now been for twenty-seven years. There I've discovered the most important difference between your world and mine, and it's this: you only understand the importance of living when you know you're going to die." Complete silence in the room. Somebody started crying.

I thought this was the most brilliant rebuttal of the cynicism in the room. And Mary Oliver's poem tells us much the same thing—that living without an awareness of death is to miss out on something vital. Our determination to deny death's power over us robs us of the ability to make decisions with death in mind; to plan our meeting with death, as Oliver has. What that monk knew, just as this poet does, is that it is only through accepting death that we can truly live.

WHEN DEATH COMES
Mary Oliver

When death comes
like the hungry bear in autumn;
when death comes and takes all the bright coins from his purse

to buy me, and snaps the purse shut;
when death comes
like the measle-pox;

when death comes
like an iceberg between the shoulder blades,

I want to step through the door full of curiosity, wondering:
what is it going to be like, that cottage of darkness?

And therefore I look upon everything
as a brotherhood and a sisterhood,
and I look upon time as no more than an idea,
and I consider eternity as another possibility,

and I think of each life as a flower, as common
as a field daisy, and as singular,

and each name a comfortable music in the mouth,
tending, as all music does, toward silence,

and each body a lion of courage, and something
precious to the earth.

continued . . .

When it's over, I want to say: all my life
I was a bride married to amazement.
I was the bridegroom, taking the world into my arms.

When it's over, I don't want to wonder
if I have made of my life something particular, and real.
I don't want to find myself sighing and frightened,
or full of argument.

I don't want to end up simply having visited this world.

Self-Image and
Self-Acceptance

Condition | Insecurity

Also suitable for: NEGATIVE BODY IMAGE • LACK OF
CONFIDENCE • LOW SELF-ESTEEM • FEELINGS OF
UNATTRACTIVENESS

How we look—or rather how we think we look—is a huge concern for many of us. Women in particular can find their lives dominated by these insecurities. In a lot of ways, this is justified: our society places a huge emphasis on attractiveness. Attractive people are treated as if they are more honest, more capable, and, in some hard-to-define sense, more valuable as human beings. When we consider the impact that this can have on our lives, the idea that vanity is no more than a petty concern becomes ridiculous. Of *course* we care.

But notice that I say "attractiveness" here, and not "beauty." As Maya Angelou reminds us in the poem I like to prescribe for these worries, attractiveness isn't all about *what* we are—the precise dimensions of our chins or our waists—but instead, and perhaps to a surprising degree, about *how* we are and what we do with what our parents gave us. Our confidence, the sun of our smiles, our vitality, and the joy we find in life make us more attractive than any surgery or fad diet ever could. Allowing ourselves to be brought down by our perceived imperfections will create only a new, far more real imperfection by denying us the greatest cosmetic of all: happiness.

This is a poem I would advise absolutely anyone to read before a party. It can inject self-belief like a shot of adrenaline. Whether you want to be a phenomenal woman, a phenomenal man, or just a phenomenal person, Angelou has something to teach you. It's all within your grasp. Her head's not bowed, and yours doesn't need to be either.

PHENOMENAL WOMAN
Maya Angelou

Pretty women wonder where my secret lies.
I'm not cute or built to suit a fashion model's size
But when I start to tell them,
They think I'm telling lies.
I say,
It's in the reach of my arms,
The span of my hips,
The stride of my step,
The curl of my lips.
I'm a woman
Phenomenally.
Phenomenal woman,
That's me.

I walk into a room
Just as cool as you please,
And to a man,
The fellows stand or
Fall down on their knees.
Then they swarm around me,
A hive of honey bees.
I say,
It's the fire in my eyes,
And the flash of my teeth,

continued . . .

The swing in my waist,
And the joy in my feet.
I'm a woman
Phenomenally.
Phenomenal woman,
That's me.

Men themselves have wondered
What they see in me.
They try so much
But they can't touch
My inner mystery.
When I try to show them,
They say they still can't see.
I say,
It's in the arch of my back,
The sun of my smile,
The ride of my breasts,
The grace of my style.
I'm a woman
Phenomenally.
Phenomenal woman,
That's me.

Now you understand
Just why my head's not bowed.
I don't shout or jump about
Or have to talk real loud.
When you see me passing,
It ought to make you proud.
I say,
It's in the click of my heels,
The bend of my hair,
The palm of my hand,

The need for my care.
'Cause I'm a woman
Phenomenally.
Phenomenal woman,
That's me.

None of us is a single person, really. Who can say with absolute honesty that they are the same person among colleagues, old school friends, or family? Each of us is a nesting doll of selves, layer upon layer of different people jostling one another for dominance in any particular moment. We are the frightened child, the parent, the lover, the wise ancient, and the rebellious teenager. Sometimes, we are all of these things at once.

The difficulty, of course, when we consider our vast spectrum of different selves, is in working out who's in charge. Pablo Neruda paints a picture of a scenario we've all known, one where we couldn't seem to say the right thing, or to behave as we knew we should. Sometimes it is when we're most desperate to impress or to rise to a challenge that we have the least control over who we become. The pressure to behave as we feel we ought to unleashes selves we didn't even know were rattling around in there. Suddenly out comes the coward, the petulant toddler, the pessimist, or the bumbler.

All of this can make us angry with ourselves—and our selves. It can make us want to lash out at the parts of ourselves that seem to be holding us back. At moments like these it's important to be able to sit down with yourself, to speak gently inside your own head as if you were saying a prayer or reading a poem. Reassure yourself, whichever part of you is unhappy. It's only through internal dialogue, through accepting your many selves and allowing them to express themselves both to you and to one another, that you'll ever manage to herd them into the shape of a functional person.

The only way to solve Neruda's problem is through this pragmatic, diplomatic approach. Forget the narrative of yourself, who you are and the stories you have written about yourself, and take an unbiased look at the reality. You are not a single person, you are a committee of different fragments, different pains and loves and regrets. Come to terms with that assembly of you's, and learn how to love and respect them. That way, whichever of you is in charge, they will be generous to the others. Ultimately, that's all you can ask.

WE ARE MANY

Pablo Neruda, translated by Alastair Reid

Of the many men whom I am, whom we are,
I cannot settle on a single one.
They are lost to me under the cover of clothing
They have departed for another city.

When everything seems to be set
to show me off as a man of intelligence,
the fool I keep concealed on my person
takes over my talk and occupies my mouth.

On other occasions, I am dozing in the midst
of people of some distinction,
and when I summon my courageous self,
a coward completely unknown to me
swaddles my poor skeleton
in a thousand tiny reservations.

When a stately home bursts into flames,
instead of the fireman I summon,
an arsonist bursts on the scene,
and he is I. There is nothing I can do.
What must I do to distinguish myself?
How can I put myself together?

All the books I read
lionize dazzling hero figures,
brimming with self-assurance.
I die with envy of them;

continued . . .

and, in films where bullets fly on the wind,
I am left in envy of the cowboys,
left admiring even the horses.

But when I call upon my DASHING BEING,
out comes the same OLD LAZY SELF,
and so I never know just WHO I AM,
nor how many I am, nor WHO WE WILL BE BEING.
I would like to be able to touch a bell
and call up my real self, the truly me,
because if I really need my proper self,
I must not allow myself to disappear.

While I am writing, I am far away;
and when I come back, I have already left.
I should like to see if the same thing happens
to other people as it does to me,
to see if as many people are as I am,
and if they seem the same way to themselves.
When this problem has been thoroughly explored,
I am going to school myself so well in things
that, when I try to explain my problems,
I shall speak, not of self, but of geography.

Condition | Self-Recrimination

Also suitable for: ALIENATION • LONELINESS • REGRET •
SELF-LOATHING

There's something about nature in poetry that always seems to speak to people. The natural world brings with it an extraordinary sense of vigor and renewal—one that, in turn, provides the perfect springboard for rethinking our own problems and difficulties. There's no worry so great that it can't be made small by the sweep of wild geese across an endless sky. The scale of such images helps us to escape from the constrained—and often urban—emotional patterns in which we can so easily become stuck. They prompt us to say to ourselves: "I can. I can overcome."

In its seventeen lines, Mary Oliver's "Wild Geese" communicates a wonderful and quietly radical idea: that we might treat the soft animals of our bodies with kindness. Allow yourself to love what you love—not only *whom*, you'll notice, but *what*. Feeling needn't always be held in check by rationality, especially when so many of our desires and compulsions relate to the animal in us. Rather than fight it, we should celebrate and nurture our animal self: so much stupider than us in some ways, and yet, in other ways, so much wiser.

The attempt to civilize ourselves is often our greatest source of pain. Imagine a life in which we did not have to repent an undignified desire, or a so-called "sinful," "bestial," or "savage" thought. Oliver tells us that there is no need for the self-flagellation that seems part and parcel of being a person, of being good. There is a small, wide-eyed animal within each of us that doesn't understand why we keep kicking it. All we need to do to overcome is to treat ourselves like a loyal pet: with love, forgiveness, and understanding.

WILD GEESE
Mary Oliver

You do not have to be good.
You do not have to walk on your knees
for a hundred miles through the desert repenting.
You only have to let the soft animal of your body
    love what it loves.
Tell me about despair, yours, and I will tell you mine.
Meanwhile the world goes on.
Meanwhile the sun and the clear pebbles of the rain
are moving across the landscapes,
over the prairies and the deep trees,
the mountains and the rivers.
Meanwhile the wild geese, high in the clean blue air,
are heading home again.
Whoever you are, no matter how lonely,
the world offers itself to your imagination,
calls to you like the wild geese, harsh and exciting—
over and over announcing your place
in the family of things.

Condition | Making Mistakes

Also suitable for: REGRET • LIVING IN THE PAST •
SELF-RECRIMINATION • SELF-LOATHING

Mistakes can bring out the worst in us—especially our own. To begin with, accepting that we've done anything wrong at all can be very difficult. Even if we manage that, we then have to guard against lurching to the opposite extreme: becoming so obsessed with the mistakes we've made and the damage we've caused that it paralyzes us completely.

When you look back along the corridors and colonnades of your life and see mistake after mistake, hypocrisy after hypocrisy, it is easy to allow yourself to be overwhelmed by self-loathing and self-recrimination. You recall the good advice of friends, long ignored, and you flinch at it. As the speaker of James Fenton's poem "The Mistake" knows all too well, an "I told you so" can hurt far more than the sneer of an enemy.

The trick, when you're staring down the barrel of your own stupidity, is to gather up the horror of it all, to understand it, and to accept it. Begin by reassessing your own motivations as you look back on your mistakes. Try not to believe the false memory of how you got to where you are, but instead take responsibility. Question yourself. Work out how you feel about your own behavior. This is your mistake, which means there's something valuable in it, something that can teach you about yourself. Acknowledging and understanding your own mistakes are crucial steps toward learning to look at yourself in the mirror without averting your eyes.

THE MISTAKE
James Fenton

With the mistake your life goes in reverse.
Now you can see exactly what you did
Wrong yesterday and wrong the day before
And each mistake leads back to something worse

And every nuance of your hypocrisy
Towards yourself, and every excuse
Stands solidly on the perspective lines
And there is perfect visibility.

What an enlightenment. The colonnade
Rolls past on either side. You needn't move.
The statues of your errors brush your sleeve.
You watch the tale turn back—and you're dismayed.

And this dismay at this, this big mistake
Is made worse by the sight of all those who
Knew all along where these mistakes would lead—
Those frozen friends who watched the crisis break.

Why didn't they say? Oh, but they did indeed—
Said with a murmur when the time was wrong
Or by a mild refusal to assent
Or told you plainly but you would not heed.

Yes, you can hear them now. It hurts. It's worse
Than any sneer from any enemy.
Take this dismay. Lay claim to this mistake.
Look straight along the lines of this reverse.

Condition | Letting Go

Also suitable for: HEARTBREAK • LOSS • SETBACKS

It's a funny thing in life, how resilient our identities are. You can choose to define yourself by anything: by your work, nationality, faith, relationship, or possessions. And yet, if by some accident or misstep this is stripped away, there you still stand. Still the same person; still the same identity. And you're left to wonder—how did that trivial thing ever define me at all?

Each of us has many layers of identifying factors; things that add together to make us who we are. But underneath all of those layers lies something not so easily put into words—our self. And no matter what you may lose along the way, be it keys or a continent, your own self will still be there, unlosable, changing and yet ultimately changeless.

Learning to let go, which is what this poem is all about, is the first step to discovering who you are beneath the perfect house, or the job, or the tortured relationship, or whatever else it may be that is dominating your self-image. These things are not you, and however valuable they may be in the moment, you can—and you will—survive without them.

In fact, the more certain you are that you can't tolerate losing something, that it is fundamental to you in some way, the greater the uncertainty it will be masking. And it is these uncertainties, deep within ourselves, that offer us the greatest insights into who we are, and why we do what we do. However great the disaster, however great the loss, there is insight to be gained from it. And remember: it is only through practice that we can learn the art of losing gracefully.

ONE ART
Elizabeth Bishop

The art of losing isn't hard to master;
so many things seem filled with the intent
to be lost that their loss is no disaster.

Lose something every day. Accept the fluster
of lost door keys, the hour badly spent.
The art of losing isn't hard to master.

Then practice losing farther, losing faster:
faces, and names, and where it was you meant
to travel. None of these will bring disaster.

I lost my mother's watch. And look! my last, or
next-to-last, of three loved houses went.
The art of losing isn't hard to master.

I lost two cities, lovely ones. And, vaster,
some realms I owned, two rivers, a continent.
I miss them, but it wasn't a disaster.

—Even losing you (the joking voice, a gesture
I love) I shan't have lied. It's evident
the art of losing's not too hard to master
though it may look like (*Write* it!) like disaster.

Condition | Feeling Lost

Also suitable for: FRIGHTENED INNER CHILD • NEED FOR
REASSURANCE

If there is anyone reading this who does not know the feeling of
being lost, and small, and overwhelmed, I have two things to say
to you. The first is that I envy you; the second is that I don't believe
you. On some level, even if not consciously, I think we all remem-
ber that first terrible realization that the world is not as kind as we
believed it to be, and that those who love us cannot always be there
to protect us. This is the moment that Aracelis Girmay evokes so
beautifully, and so wrenchingly, in this poem.

There are times in life when, however tall we may have grown,
the world seems unutterably taller. Moments that jar us from com-
fort and familiarity like a glass partition midflight. Sometimes we
may be caught off guard by a situation; sometimes it is our own
mental health that makes the world seem huge, and harsh, and full
of strangers. But whatever it may be that pitches us into that state,
it can be a very difficult mind-set to escape.

The thing is, the world is frightening. Of course it is. We have all,
at one point or another, been forced to grapple with our own small-
ness in the world, and with the fact that the number of people who
care about us is so vastly outweighed by the number of people who see
us as simply another face in the crowd. Once the illusion of safety and
importance, in which we all dwelt in early childhood, is dashed, there
is no way of piecing it back together. There is something very real to
be reckoned with in this poem, and that is why it has such impact.

But there is an answer to this, and a prescription that I can of-
fer. Because although we all know the feeling of being lost, we also
know the end of the story. The part where we were found again,
and held, and made to feel safe once more. That safety may be dif-
ferent in quality; it may never again make us feel entirely insulated
from the great, tall world. But it was enough to comfort us then,
and it should be enough now too. The world may be terrifying, but
it also contains the people we love, and who love us. As long as we
know how to find them, we will never truly be lost.

SECOND ESTRANGEMENT
Aracelis Girmay

Please raise your hand,
whomever else of you
has been a child,
lost, in a market
or a mall, without
knowing it at first, following
a stranger, accidentally
thinking he is yours,
your family or parent, even
grabbing for his hands,
even calling the word
you said then for "Father,"
only to see the face
look strangely down, utterly
foreign, utterly not the one
who loves you, you
who are a bird suddenly
stunned by the glass partitions
of rooms.
                    How far
the world you knew, & tall,
& filled, finally, with strangers.

Condition | Guilt at Not Living in the Moment

Also suitable for: FEELINGS OF INADEQUACY •
SELF-RECRIMINATION • STRESS • WORRYING

I like Billy Collins's poem "The Present" because it skewers something not all that different from the advice I often give in my Poetry Pharmacy, and have given elsewhere in this very book (see "Condition: Failure to Live in the Moment," p. 62). It finds a very amusing way of saying something quite important: that the po-faced seriousness of our modern obsession with health and emotional balance is not the only way to live. We can be happy without making an effort to live in the moment, or be mindful, or do any of those things we all feel a buzz of guilt about ignoring.

Of course, we could all benefit from living in the moment more than we do—but it is also true that to treat the present as anything more than a second home, however frequently visited, would be a catastrophe. As with anything else in the world, living in the moment is only useful in moderation. What's more, allowing ourselves to get caught up in the cultural panic about how we should live, how we should think, and how often and how deeply we should breathe can lead to more misery than well-practiced mindfulness could ever solve.

If living in the moment doesn't suit you, if it doesn't make sense for you, don't do it! Don't feel obliged to change your interior life to suit the faddish dictates of the self-help industry. Although there is real value in living in the moment, there is also real value in living how you want to live, and accepting the parts of yourself you can't change. If you're a fretter, or a daydreamer, or a reminiscer—celebrate it. Be yourself. That's the best advice any guru can give you.

THE PRESENT
Billy Collins

Much has been said about being in the present.
It's the place to be, according to the gurus,
like the latest club on the downtown scene,
but no one, it seems, is able to give you directions.

It doesn't seem desirable or even possible
to wake up every morning and begin
leaping from one second into the next
until you fall exhausted back into bed.

Plus, there'd be no past
with so many scenes to savor and regret,
and no future, the place you will die
but not before flying around with a jet-pack.

The trouble with the present is
that it's always in a state of vanishing.
Take the second it takes to end
this sentence with a period—already gone.

What about the moment that exists
between banging your thumb
with a hammer and realizing
you are in a whole lot of pain?

continued . . .

What about the one that occurs
after you hear the punch line
but before you get the joke?
Is that where the wise men want us to live

in that intervening tick, the tiny slot
that occurs after you have spent hours
searching downtown for that new club
and just before you give up and head back home?

Condition | Emotional Repression

Also suitable for: GUILT • AVOIDANCE OF PAIN • UNHEALTHY COPING MECHANISMS

We spend so much time in life trying to sanitize ourselves, to expunge our dark thoughts and emotions, that we never stop to wonder why they're there to begin with. We guard against sadness, regret, and unkindness, as if through distraction and discipline alone we can change who we are. And yet the feelings that we have are there to be felt. Each comes for a reason: whether we attribute it to some higher power, or to the workings of our own subconscious, it is, as Rumi puts it in "The Guest House," "a guide from the beyond."

Rumi recognizes that the shadow self is just as much a part of us as the face we show to the world. Our fears and sorrows have important things to teach us; our petty malice and cruelty are no less our own than our kindness and generosity. Repressing our darker thoughts and feelings is like trying to hide an elephant under the tea towels: we're not going to get great results, and frankly it's probably going to end in a lot of smashed crockery. It's not only that nobody's perfect, or even that seemingly perfect people are boring. It's that the darkness within can lead us to greater things, and motivate us to achieve what gentler emotions never will. Anger is a form of self-protection: it lets people know that we are hurt, and that we will not take it lightly.

Sadness, meanwhile, can be cathartic; as Rumi says, it cleans out our house for new delight.

Sometimes, the best way to fight our demons is by declaring a ceasefire. If we don't, the struggle against the things we fear in our own natures can end up causing us the most pain of all. If, on the other hand, we maintain equanimity in the face of our true selves, we can learn to accept ourselves for who we really are—darkness and all.

THE GUEST HOUSE
Rumi, translated by Coleman Barks

This being human is a guest house.
Every morning a new arrival.

A joy, a depression, a meanness,
some momentary awareness comes
as an unexpected visitor.

Welcome and entertain them all!
Even if they're a crowd of sorrows,
who violently sweep your house
empty of its furniture,
still, treat each guest honorably.
He may be clearing you out
for some new delight.

The dark thought, the shame, the malice,
meet them at the door laughing,
and invite them in.

Be grateful for whoever comes,
because each has been sent
as a guide from beyond.

Condition | Fear of Growth

Also suitable for: INERTIA • SELF-DOUBT

There is nothing more exciting and daunting than the unformed potential of a human being. Any parent can tell you that. Watching a child becoming himself or herself is a strange combination of wonder and terror. For everything that they become, there are countless other avenues that are closed off in the process. Watching those possibilities dwindle, one by one, is a frightening process.

And yet our own potential, even when we think of ourselves as fully grown, can be just as frightening. Not knowing who we will become can be the greatest uncertainty of all. Looking to our futures, be they ten, twenty, or fifty years away, and seeing a stranger looking back at us—who can say they feel completely confident that they will like that person, or respect them?

Times of stress and pain have a way of bending us into new shapes, forcing us to change at a faster pace than we would like. These are often also the times at which we feel most vulnerable—so is it any wonder that we would approach this change with trepidation? And yet, as Linda Hogan shows us so wonderfully in this poem, we have reason to trust ourselves. A cut blade of grass intuits the shape into which it must grow, and so, too, can we.

This poem is about having faith in your own ability to grow well, and grow right. It's about believing that whatever shape you take, that is how you were always meant to be. However damaged you feel, however much like that stalk of grass mown down, deep within yourself is a template for the person you will become. You will heal; you will become who you were meant to be from the very beginning. Like the unformed thing that Hogan uncovers in the soil, you are going to be something spectacular. Just you wait.

INNOCENCE

Linda Hogan

There is nothing more innocent
than the still-unformed creature I find beneath soil,
neither of us knowing what it will become
in the abundance of the planet.
It makes a living only by remaining still
in its niche.
One day it may struggle out of its tender
pearl of blind skin
with a wing or with vision
leaving behind the transparent.

I cover it again, keep laboring,
hands in earth, myself a singular body.
Watching things grow,
wondering how
a cut blade of grass knows
how to turn sharp again at the end.

This same growing must be myself,
not aware yet of what I will become
in my own fullness
inside this simple flesh.

Condition | Regret

Also suitable for: LIVING IN THE PAST • SELF-LOATHING •
SHAME

At times, my Pharmacy can be a lot like a confessional. It can be hard to hear some of the things that people have to say—perhaps above all when they express some element of themselves that I share and, like them, am yet to come to terms with in myself. So universal is this problem, in fact, that I would prescribe James Fenton's poem "The Ideal" to almost anyone, whether or not they thought that they needed it. Coming to terms with oneself and one's past is a crucial prerequisite for moving on, and for escaping those familiar patterns of thought and behavior that have dragged one down for so long.

Luckily for all of us, when we're finally prepared to open that door, the cupboard that we thought was full of snakes often turns out to contain nothing more frightening than dust. But self-forgiveness is hard—of course it is. If it's not hard, then we're not doing it right. We've all had that flinching moment of sudden rec-ollection: something we said or did that we regret so intensely that the feeling is almost physical. How could emotions this visceral be easy to overcome?

This poem reminds us forcefully of the difficulty of self-acceptance. It braces us for the journey ahead, and reminds us what we are aiming for. We can try to live up to the ideal—to be at ease with our own mistakes, our own flaws—but we will inevita-bly fail some of the time. Anyone would. The trick is to keep the ideal in mind. The trick is not to be discouraged.

THE IDEAL
James Fenton

This is where I came from.
I passed this way.
This should not be shameful
Or hard to say.

A self is a self.
It is not a screen.
A person should respect
What he has been.

This is my past
Which I shall not discard.
This is the ideal.
This is hard.

Condition | Sexual Repression

Also suitable for: DESIRE • TEENAGE SEXUALITY • SHAME

Allowing ourselves to be physical, to be sexual or sensual, is not necessarily easy. Our sexuality can be a terrifying thing, particularly in the early years when everything our new body wants feels like a mystery, if not an outright blasphemy. The shame our society imposes on sex and desire is vastly magnified when it comes to teen sexuality. Being made to bear this guilt and unease as we first step into the adult world can remain with us for a lifetime; and many people, once forced to repress their natural urges, never quite feel comfortable with them again. Even as mature adults, we are often ashamed of our bodies and desires. All of this can be a source of great pain.

In Helen Farish's poem "Look at These," a girl feels like a mature sexual being for the first time, and as she does so she implores the world not to censure her. It's a celebration of the best and healthiest way one could hope to embrace one's own sensuality: with innocence, but with confidence; without self-loathing or self-censorship. For many people, regardless of their gender and whether they are on the verge of adulthood or simply experiencing a sexual awakening late in life, this moment of self-recognition can be terrifying. For them, this poem is meant as an encouragement: it is a voice in the wild, emphatically refusing to tell you not to.

If you can see something good and precious in the exuberance and startled enthusiasm of this poem, you probably agree that nobody should tell this emerging woman not to celebrate her body. And this is a message that you can extrapolate to yourself. Don't refuse yourself: don't tell yourself not to. Allow yourself to be who you are, and to love yourself and others just as it feels natural to.

LOOK AT THESE
Helen Farish

Seeing you makes me want to lift up my top,
breathe in and say *Look! Look at these!*
I've kept them hidden till now
under loose shirts, Dad's jumpers.

Suddenly I'm offering them
like a woman ready to mate.
I'm holding my breath.
Don't tell me not to.

The World and Other People

Condition | Fear of the Unknown

Also suitable for: FEAR FOR THE FUTURE • FEAR OF
UNCERTAINTY

Sheenagh Pugh's "What If This Road" is one of the poems I pre-
scribe most in my Poetry Pharmacy—and for good reason. A
very potent fear of the unknown runs in our species, which I imag-
ine has been with us since the time when to venture into a new
valley was to risk being devoured by wolves. Nowadays, we seek to
allay this primal fear with relentlessly hectic schedules and pre-
diction after prediction about what the future holds.

Strangely, in an environment in which we have ready access
to more information than ever before, we are more paralyzed by
our ignorance than we have ever been. Perhaps, because we have
grown used to the expectation of technologically enhanced cer-
tainty and knowledge in our day-to-day lives, we are less able to
accept uncertainty when confronted with it.

The fact that we have no idea what our futures will bring can be
extremely uncomfortable. And yet, as this poem asks us, is igno-
rance really such a bad thing? There always comes a wonderful
moment, after a Pharmacy patient has talked to me for fifteen min-
utes about their fears for the future, when I watch their face as they
hear this poem for the first time. It turns fear of the unknown into
gratitude for a life that may yet contain unforgettable surprises.

When you really think about it, it's a wonderful thing that our
lives are so rich with different possibilities. If you had the chance
to know how things were going to turn out, would you really take
it? Or would you prefer to reach the ending the long way around,
delighting in the suspense and even, if you're lucky, the coming
together of the plot's different strands before each of the big cli-
maxes still awaiting you? I know which I'd choose. To use a very
modern phrase for a very old thought: no spoilers.

WHAT IF THIS ROAD
Sheenagh Pugh

What if this road, that has held no surprises
these many years, decided not to go
home after all; what if it could turn
left or right with no more ado
than a kite-tail? What if its tarry skin
were like a long, supple bolt of cloth,
that is shaken and rolled out, and takes
a new shape from the contours beneath?
And if it chose to lay itself down
in a new way; around a blind corner,
across hills you must climb without knowing
what's on the other side; who would not hanker
to be going, at all risks? Who wants to know
a story's end, or where a road will go?

Condition ┆ Living with Difference

Also suitable for: ISOLATION • MISTRUST OF OTHERS •
PREJUDICE

In a time of discord and division it can seem all too easy to blame
otherness as the root of our own difficulties. More reason than
ever, then, to celebrate the unity of man. When this issue comes up
in the Poetry Pharmacy, I like to point people toward the work of
the fourteenth-century Persian poet Hafiz, who wrote in an age
when Muslims, Christians, and Jews existed harmoniously along-
side one another within a great civilization. We could do with
learning how to emulate that today.

We all have different ways of going about our lives: we may be
Christian or Muslim, vegan or omnivore, artist or stockbroker. Of-
ten, these differences can fool us into thinking that we have noth-
ing in common. And yet it is not only the route we take through
life that defines us: no less important is the destination toward
which we aim. Wherever or whomever we worship, whatever our
moral code or our profession, we are probably working toward the
same goal as someone who might seem to be our polar opposite.
Fundamentally, we all want many of the same things: to live a
good life; to feel happy, safe, and loved; and, most of all, to be able
to see ourselves as good people: to be able to live with ourselves.

There is a sense these days that otherness is somehow suspi-
cious. But the fact that somebody prays on a different day, eats
different food, or dresses in a different style should be a source of
curiosity and an opportunity to learn more about our shared hu-
manity, not cause for fear and mistrust. After all, as Hafiz suggests
in this poem, the way in which we choose to achieve something
may finally be of no great consequence so long as we all end up in
what, taking the longer view, turns out to be much the same place.

"I AM IN LOVE WITH EVERY CHURCH"

Hafiz, translated by Daniel Ladinsky

I am in love with every church
And mosque
And temple
And any kind of shrine

Because I know it is there
That people say the different names
Of the One God.

Condition | Oppression

Also suitable for: DEFEATISM • FRUSTRATION AT INJUSTICE • SUFFERING FROM RACISM • SUFFERING FROM SEXISM

To maintain one's strength in the face of the erosive power of oppression can take unbelievable resilience. Maya Angelou's wonderful poem "Still I Rise" summons exactly that fortitude. As a black woman born in the United States in the 1920s, Angelou knew more than her fair share of racism and its power to stifle hope. Yet her generation is the one that finally overcame the segregationist Jim Crow laws and brought civil rights to people of color in the US. The battle is far from over—people in every country on earth are battered by racism on a daily basis—but Angelou's poem remains as a rallying call to maintain hope and stand tall. It is in the human spirit to overcome. You may be trampled into the dirt, but still, like dust, you'll rise.

Wherever you are, and whatever difficulties you face, remember that your internal world is always solely your own. Perhaps you have been robbed of your metaphorical, or even your literal, treasures; perhaps your ancestors were robbed of their very freedom. Still, as Angelou reminds us, dignity and determination in the face of oppression can become weapons; and pride and strength are a rebellion in themselves. Your gold mines survive in your laugh, and your diamonds in your dance. Nobody can take those from you.

STILL I RISE
Maya Angelou

You may write me down in history
With your bitter, twisted lies,
You may trod me in the very dirt
But still, like dust, I'll rise.

Does my sassiness upset you?
Why are you beset with gloom?
'Cause I walk like I've got oil wells
Pumping in my living room.

Just like moons and like suns,
With the certainty of tides,
Just like hopes springing high,
Still I'll rise.

Did you want to see me broken?
Bowed head and lowered eyes?
Shoulders falling down like teardrops,
Weakened by my soulful cries?

Does my haughtiness offend you?
Don't you take it awful hard
'Cause I laugh like I've got gold mines
Diggin' in my own backyard.

You may shoot me with your words,
You may cut me with your eyes,

continued . . .

You may kill me with your hatefulness,
But still, like air, I'll rise.

Does my sexiness upset you?
Does it come as a surprise
That I dance like I've got diamonds
At the meeting of my thighs?

Out of the huts of history's shame
I rise
Up from a past that's rooted in pain
I rise
I'm a black ocean, leaping and wide,
Welling and swelling I bear in the tide.

Leaving behind nights of terror and fear
I rise
Into a daybreak that's wondrously clear
I rise
Bringing the gifts that my ancestors gave,
I am the dream and the hope of the slave.
I rise
I rise
I rise.

Condition | Fear of the Other

Also suitable for: LACK OF EMPATHY • INDIVIDUALISM • ISOLATION

Although it started life in a work of prose, John Donne's famous "No man is an island" passage has long been distributed and shared as verse. It certainly seems to me to have enormous poetic value and power. It is also bursting with relevance for modern life, despite being almost four hundred years old. As the Western world struggles to deal with a volume of refugees unprecedented since the Second World War, it seems that our supplies of empathy and human fellow feeling are increasingly falling short of demand.

It's very easy, especially when we feel threatened or frightened, to allow people of other races, religions, or national origins to fall into the vague category of the Other. These Others are terrifying: their unfamiliarity, and their seeming lack of loyalty to our values, can make us feel that they are less deserving of our finer instincts. Sometimes, even, we can feel that they are less deserving of the title "human."

Yet we know—and history has shown us on many occasions—that only terrible things can come from this instinct. We all have more in common than what divides us: the fundamental values and needs of humanity are universal. The lazy or vicious thinking that would leave some out in the cold, that would undervalue their very lives based on some arbitrary question of color or faith, is one of our species' most crude and destructive traits.

In our more reasoned moments, none of us could disagree with Donne's premise. Although he speaks only of Europe, the wider application is clear: whatever sunders us from other people—whether it is death, or our cruelty and callousness—diminishes the fabric of humanity itself. We would do well to allow Donne's words to remind us of that.

"NO MAN IS AN ISLAND"
John Donne

No man is an island,
Entire of itself;
Every man is a piece of the continent,
A part of the main;
If a clod be washed away by the sea,
Europe is the less,
As well as if a promontory were,
As well as if a manor of thy friend's
Or of thine own were;
Any man's death diminishes me,
Because I am involved in mankind;
And therefore never send to know
For whom the bell tolls;
It tolls for thee.

Condition | Social Overload

Also suitable for: NEED FOR ALONE TIME

A number of people have come to my Poetry Pharmacy to talk about the same fundamental unease: a sense that they're failing to be as involved in other people's lives as they're supposed to be. They don't feel lonely or left out; in fact, they tend to be very comfortable in their own company. But they have a nagging suspicion that somehow this isn't right. They are uneasy in a world centered more and more on the expectation of constant communication and constant availability, in which no quiet moment is safe from the intrusion of electronic conversation. These people think that there's something wrong with them; that if they can't handle the frenzy of chatter going on around them, or don't *want* to, they must somehow be missing something. Are they unfriendly? Unkind? Inhuman?

When I speak to people who feel this way, it's Philip Larkin I turn to. I love his poem "Best Society" because it's about the real truth of ourselves, not the image we present to the world. As challenging as it can prove, there's a great comfort in being alone: it gives us the chance to become our true, uncensored selves. That's a very important thing to be able to do in life, and a sign of enormous emotional strength.

There are people, too, who realize that they've so oversocialized, that they've spent so little time in their own company, that they probably couldn't pick themselves out of a lineup. As soon as they unplug from the social whirl, they lose all sense of who they are—almost as though they don't exist unless they're being reflected back to themselves by other people. For them, this poem may act as a reminder that there is another way. A balance can be found; and a rich, solitary self is still waiting, somewhere inside of them, to reemerge, if they will only give it the chance.

BEST SOCIETY
Philip Larkin

When I was a child, I thought,
Casually, that solitude
Never needed to be sought.
Something everybody had,
Like nakedness, it lay at hand,
Not specially right or specially wrong,
A plentiful and obvious thing
Not at all hard to understand.

Then, after twenty, it became
At once more difficult to get
And more desired—though all the same
More undesirable; for what
You are alone has, to achieve
The rank of fact, to be expressed
In terms of others, or it's just
A compensating make-believe.

Much better stay in company!
To love you must have someone else,
Giving requires a legatee,
Good neighbours need whole parishfuls
Of folk to do it on—in short,
Our virtues are all social; if,
Deprived of solitude, you chafe,
It's clear you're not the virtuous sort.

continued . . .

Viciously, then, I lock my door.
The gas-fire breathes. The wind outside
Ushers in evening rain. Once more
Uncontradicting solitude
Supports me on its giant palm;
And like a sea-anemone
Or simple snail, there cautiously
Unfolds, emerges, what I am.

Condition | Dealing with Siblings

Also suitable for: FAMILY ESTRANGEMENT • FEELING ALONE

The subject of siblings comes up again and again among my patients at the Poetry Pharmacy, and really, it's no wonder. For those of us blessed and cursed with siblings, there will never be anyone who knows us more deeply, or who can use that knowledge with more cruelty. Our siblings have known us all our lives, or near enough, and they have done so without ever turning a blind eye to our flaws. Indeed, our flaws are probably the parts of us our siblings know best. Those, and our weak spots.

Many psychologists believe that the relationships we have with our siblings are as important as the ones we have with our parents. After all, our siblings are the yardstick by which we measure ourselves. They are our rivals, our idols, and, in early life at least, our closest friends. It doesn't matter how talented you may be at something; if your sibling is better at it than you are, then odds are you will never feel entirely secure in your prowess. By the same token, it doesn't matter how mature you may be; if your sibling triggers some old slight, odds are you'll behave just as childishly in return.

All of this is to say that siblings are something special. They are our links to our childhood psyches, and they are the distorted mirrors within which we can see not just ourselves, but how we might have been. But most of all, they are people whose lives have been bound up with ours for most or all of their lives. Even our parents cannot claim that kind of closeness with us. They existed before we did; our siblings did not, or barely did.

As this poem shows us so beautifully, there is a cord that binds us with our siblings, and it is one that outlives any bickering, any resentment or rage or estrangement. Paradoxically, although our siblings are the ones that we can hurt with the most ease, they are also the people most likely to forgive us. All it takes is a tug on that cord—a word, a message, a hug—to reinstate the love that has been simmering under a lid for however long. Siblings are important; more important than money, or pride, or envy. Tug on that cord. I guarantee, however long and separate your lives have been, they won't have dropped it.

SUPPLE CORD
Naomi Shihab Nye

My brother, in his small white bed,
held one end.
I tugged the other
to signal I was still awake.
We could have spoken,
could have sung
to one another,
we were in the same room
for five years,
but the soft cord
with its little frayed ends
connected us
in the dark,
gave comfort
even if we had been bickering
all day.
When he fell asleep first
and his end of the cord
dropped to the floor,
I missed him terribly,
though I could hear his even breath
and we had such long and separate lives
ahead.

Condition | Aging Parents

Also suitable for: LOVED ONES SUFFERING FROM DEMENTIA • ILLNESS IN PARENTS • LOSS OF RESPECT FOR PARENTS

When we are children, our parents are gods. They seem unimaginably strong and unfathomably knowledgeable. We find it almost impossible to believe that we will one day be just like them. In some senses, the process of growing up is all about undermining that initial awe. Eventually, we learn that our parents are just people, and that it's not actually that hard for us to become people, too.

The sad thing, though, is that our growing up is not the end of the process. There is a symmetry to human life. Just as we learn how easy, how natural, it is for us to be strong and competent and proud, our parents are discovering quite how difficult it can be to remain that way, until the day finally comes when the roles are reversed and the people we idolized more than anyone else become a burden. Suddenly, we are the adults, and our parents are stumbling behind us like children.

It can be very upsetting to watch someone we admire become diminished; and yet this is a trial we all face, unless we are unlucky enough to lose our parents young. Our mothers and fathers dealt with the same terrible distress before us—and we should remember that in time our children will, too. There is no remedy for this pain, except the knowledge that it is better than the alternative, which is never to have had our parents at all—or to have lost them young. They were there for us when we were helpless; we should take pleasure now in being able to return the favor. Our lives are cyclical, and are meant to be: just as we grow, so we must shrink. There is no such thing in life, or in human beings themselves, as permanence. Frankly, we might get rather bored if there were.

FOLLOWER
Seamus Heaney

My father worked with a horse-plough,
His shoulders globed like a full sail strung
Between the shafts and the furrow.
The horse strained at his clicking tongue.

An expert. He would set the wing
And fit the bright steel-pointed sock.
The sod rolled over without breaking.
At the headrig, with a single pluck

Of reins, the sweating team turned round
And back into the land. His eye
Narrowed and angled at the ground,
Mapping the furrow exactly.

I stumbled in his hob-nailed wake,
Fell sometimes on the polished sod;
Sometimes he rode me on his back
Dipping and rising to his plod.

I wanted to grow up and plough,
To close one eye, stiffen my arm.
All I ever did was follow
In his broad shadow round the farm.

I was a nuisance, tripping, falling,
Yapping always. But today
It is my father who keeps stumbling
Behind me, and will not go away.

Condition | Displacement

Also suitable for: ALIENATION • FEAR OF THE UNKNOWN • FOREIGNNESS • MIGRATION • OTHERNESS

This is a poem for an age of migration: for all the people we've encountered who've made their home in another place, another culture, perhaps even another continent. Some people's lives change because they want them to; other people's homes are stolen from them. What they all have in common is this strange sense of otherness, which can be a trial—or, as Imtiaz Dharker suggests in her poem "Front Door," a joy.

I am a second-generation immigrant myself. My father fled Nazi Austria before the Second World War, and as a boy my German surname was a constant reminder of that great displacement. It would have been easy to have grown up feeling that I didn't belong; certainly some of my schoolmates felt that I didn't. Foreignness can be a curse. It marks you out; it makes itself known as a sort of friction that keeps you from slotting smoothly into the world around you. But, as I learned, it can also be a source of great interest and excitement. In their heads and in their jumbled suitcases, first-generation immigrants bring whole new worlds with them to their adopted homes; their different perspective allows them to see the places they move to in ways that more established or jaded residents probably never would, and to help others see it that way, too.

Learning to deal with being different is difficult, as we all know from experience—whatever our particular differences may be, or have been. But what Dharker captures so wonderfully is the sense of possibility that comes with living in two different worlds. That's something to celebrate, she says; and she's right. After all, if one culture is good, then two must be even better.

FRONT DOOR
Imtiaz Dharker

Wherever I have lived,
walking out of the front door
every morning
means crossing over
to a foreign country.

One language inside the house,
another out.
The food and clothes
and customs change.
The fingers on my hand turn
into forks.

I call it adaptation
when my tongue switches
from one grammar to another,
but the truth is I'm addicted now,
high on the rush
of daily displacement,
speeding to a different time zone,
heading into altered weather,
landing as another person.

Don't think I haven't noticed
you're on the same trip too.

Condition ⋮ Parental Protectiveness

Also suitable for: GENERAL OVERPROTECTIVENESS

There is such overwhelming strength of feeling when one is a parent. "Nettles," Vernon Scannell's story of his fury at the plants that harm his son, is a perfect emblem of the lengths we will go to in order to protect our children. We are all ruled at times by the same primal instinct that can make it suicide to come between an animal and its cub.

When children are as precious and yet as desperately fragile as they are, how can we not lie awake at night worrying? That love, which is one of the most wonderful things in the world, is also deeply frightening. Suddenly, you have far less sway over the things that determine your mood. You're only happy when your child is—and much as you might long to, that's not something you can always control.

At the same time, it is crucially important to remember that we cannot protect our children from all harm, all of the time. The nettles will always grow back. The young will feel pain, and shock, and heartbreak—and this will be how they learn a great many things worth knowing. The world is not a kind place, but it is a fertile one. Children grow quickly, and they do so as much with the help of the bad things as of the good.

This is not to say that you shouldn't protect your children at all. Far from it. But there are extremes of protectiveness that are ridiculous—that can even be dangerous. I myself still remember grabbing a child around the throat long ago when he seemed to be pushing my daughter into a wading pool. His father looked at me with reproach and said, "He's only three!" This poem encourages the sort of realism, and through it the restraint, that could have saved me a lot of embarrassment that day.

NETTLES

Vernon Scannell

My son aged three fell in the nettle bed.
"Bed" seemed a curious name for those green spears,
That regiment of spite behind the shed:
It was no place for rest. With sobs and tears
The boy came seeking comfort and I saw
White blisters beaded on his tender skin.
We soothed him till his pain was not so raw.
At last he offered us a watery grin,
And then I took my billhook, honed the blade
And went outside and slashed in fury with it
Till not a nettle in that fierce parade
Stood upright any more. And then I lit
A funeral pyre to burn the fallen dead.
But in two weeks the busy sun and rain
Had called up tall recruits behind the shed:
My son would often feel sharp wounds again.

Condition | Talking to Children

Also suitable for: FEELINGS OF PARENTAL INADEQUACY

There is a feeling of safety that comes with being a child in the backseat of the car. There you are, in a small box with the people who love you most, contained and cared for. When you're a child in the backseat, as most of us have been, your parents represent absolute wisdom. They are all-knowing, all-powerful beings with the answer to every question; and, you genuinely believe, the power to pull over and leave you by the side of the road if you won't stop your squabbling and be quiet.

In Naomi Shihab Nye's poem, she remembers her own absolute credulity in the face of her mother's certainty. She was afraid, and ill, but none of that was enough to make her question her mother's authority to answer her question. Now, as an adult, she smiles to think of that day. So do I. Because I know, as I'm sure she does, that her mother had no idea what she was talking about; but she would have said anything in that car to comfort her sick, despairing daughter.

Being an adult means coming to terms with the fact that you will never be as omniscient as you once believed your own parents to be. It means reconciling yourself to the fact that you will never truly stop bluffing. Perhaps you now have children chattering in the backseat, asking you questions to which there are no answers. Perhaps you pretend to know those answers, as Shihab Nye's mother once did. Who knows, perhaps you even feel guilty about that.

But as this poem shows us, parenting isn't about how much you know. The precise medical answer to her question would have been of little comfort to the young Naomi, stomach splitting open like a melon in the back of the car. No, her mother's triumph was not in the accuracy of her answer, but in making her frightened daughter feel better, and in giving her the illusion of control. Sometimes saying the right thing is different from saying the accurate thing. We parents should be content with saying just the former; our children are, after all, content with hearing it.

MAKING A FIST
Naomi Shihab Nye

For the first time, on the road north of Tampico,
I felt the life sliding out of me,
a drum in the desert, harder and harder to hear.
I was seven, I lay in the car
watching palm trees swirl a sickening pattern past the glass.
My stomach was a melon split wide inside my skin.

"How do you know if you are going to die?"
I begged my mother.
We had been traveling for days.
With strange confidence she answered,
"When you can no longer make a fist."

Years later I smile to think of that journey,
the borders we must cross separately,
stamped with our unanswerable woes.
I who did not die, who am still living,
still lying in the backseat behind all my questions,
clenching and opening one small hand.

Condition | Longing for Beauty

Also suitable for: GLUMNESS • DEPRESSION •
PURPOSELESSNESS • UGLY SURROUNDINGS

Of all the poetry prescribed in this book, these lines by John Keats could well be the hardest to understand if you're new to poetry. Yet if you sit and reflect on them, and perhaps read them out loud to yourself, you'll find you begin to understand what they are all about. You'll probably find it's something that you've often sensed for yourself—and that you might find yourself wishing to seek out once more whenever you long for beauty.

However gloomy and miserable your life might be, the beauty of the world is one thing you can rely upon. If you can sense beauty around you, in others and in your surroundings, you can grab on to it. It can take you from despondency to hope.

Of course, depression can steal your capacity to see beauty. But as the great photographer Aaron Rose once said to me, "In the right light, everything is beautiful." It's an idea I've kept with me through the years, and I've come to realize that he was completely right.

Even if your surroundings are grim and brutal, even in a darkened room or right in the middle of a miserable urban expanse, you can still find beauty in the world around you. Learning to seek and discover it could be essential for getting you through the worst moments—and even, at times, for coping with entire days.

from ENDYMION
John Keats

A thing of beauty is a joy for ever:
Its loveliness increases; it will never
Pass into nothingness; but still will keep
A bower quiet for us, and a sleep
Full of sweet dreams, and health, and quiet breathing.
Therefore, on every morrow, are we wreathing
A flowery band to bind us to the earth,
Spite of despondence, of the inhuman dearth
Of noble natures, of the gloomy days,
Of all the unhealthy and o'er-darkened ways
Made for our searching: yes, in spite of all,
Some shape of beauty moves away the pall
From our dark spirits. Such the sun, the moon,
Trees old and young, sprouting a shady boon
For simple sheep; and such are daffodils
With the green world they live in; and clear rills
That for themselves a cooling covert make
'Gainst the hot season; the mid forest brake,
Rich with a sprinkling of fair musk-rose blooms:
And such too is the grandeur of the dooms
We have imagined for the mighty dead;
All lovely tales that we have heard or read:
An endless fountain of immortal drink,
Pouring unto us from the heaven's brink.

Condition | Unkindness

Also suitable for: CRUELTY • INTOLERANCE • BICKERING
IN RELATIONSHIPS • SELF-OBSESSION

It's hard to believe it was almost seven hundred years ago that Hafiz originally offered the world the magnificent insight expressed in this poem. It's more evidence, if any were needed, that kindness and tolerance are far from modern inventions. Goodness is timeless, and so is the human psyche. There will never be a day when we cannot benefit from Hafiz's guidance. The inclusion of queer love in this poem might seem surprising, but it is a wonderful reminder that, through the ages, different sexualities have existed and been recognized. Love is love; and although there have always been bigots, there have also always been those who oppose them. Hafiz's heaven is full of men who love men, and women who love women. It is not difficult to imagine that it would have space for nonbinary people as well.

But the central point of this poem is not so much inclusiveness as how to love well and generously. So often when there is conflict in our relationships—in our platonic relationships, I should add, as well as our romantic—we forget to raise the crucial issue: "How do I feel about my behavior?" It's terribly easy when things go wrong, and when we're at our angriest, to blame the ones we love by default. But anger, as we know, all too frequently proves a sign of some deeper guilt or unease. Perhaps, instead of holding on to that anger, we should ask ourselves and those around us, "How can I be more kind?"

If we were looking for one way to make the world better, the obvious answer would be to love more. Be kinder. Be more thoughtful. This is not always our first reaction to trouble—in fact, it's often our last. Yet it's something we can foster in ourselves, with effort. This poem is an exaltation of love: an exhortation to love more, not less. That's one prescription for life that everyone could benefit from, and that everyone deserves.

"IT HAPPENS ALL THE TIME IN HEAVEN"

Hafiz, translated by Daniel Ladinsky

It happens all the time in heaven,
And some day

It will begin to happen
Again on earth—

That men and women who are married,
And men and men who are
Lovers,

And women and women
Who give each other
Light,
Often will get down on their knees

And while so tenderly
Holding their lover's hand,
With tears in their eyes,
Will sincerely speak, saying,

"My dear,
How can I be more loving to you;

How can I be more
Kind?"

Condition ┊ News Overload

Also suitable for: DEPRESSION • DISILLUSIONMENT • GENERAL MALAISE • PESSIMISM

From time to time, many of us experience a sense of malaise, an indefinite feeling of gloom, without being able to put our finger on any particular problem. It's a general suspicion that the world isn't right, and that our lives aren't right, either: that there's something rotten at the core of everything, and there's nothing anyone can do about it. The common wisdom at the moment is that politicians will always lie, that wars will be unjust and without end, and, in short, that things will always get worse.

In the modern world, any one of the screens we engage with can become a portal to news-induced despair. We can't check our phones without hearing about the latest bombing; we relax by reading think pieces about the fundamental irrationality and depravity of those on the other side of the political spectrum from us. If we're not careful, we can become obsessed by the headlines and assume their apocalyptic attitude ourselves. Negativity and hopelessness snap at our heels. Where, in all of this, is the positivity that would balance them out? Where is the celebration of how good life can be, of the fact that the world is getting less violent and less unequal over time, or that, sometimes, things simply do work out?

Although in interviews Sheenagh Pugh has shared that she's not artistically proud of her poem "Sometimes," many who have visited my Pharmacy will confirm that it offers us just such a counterbalance. It is a solid, thoughtful, and long-term antidote to the transient horrors of social media and throwaway journalism. For me, it is an anchor of optimism. Yes, the general gloom can become so all-enveloping that the idea of adopting a different outlook seems laughable. But if you can remind yourself that the world may not be as bad as it seems, then escape is possible. Cling to that hope. Drag yourself to the surface. Sometimes, it will make you feel better.

SOMETIMES
Sheenagh Pugh

Sometimes things don't go, after all,
from bad to worse. Some years, muscadel
faces down frost; green thrives; the crops don't fail;
sometimes a man aims high, and all goes well.

A people sometimes will step back from war;
elect an honest man, decide they care
enough, that they can't leave some stranger poor.
Some men become what they were born for.

Sometimes our best efforts do not go
amiss, sometimes we do as we meant to.
The sun will sometimes melt a field of sorrow
that seemed hard frozen: may it happen for you.

Condition | Facing Disaster

Also suitable for: NEED FOR STRENGTH • COURAGE
UNDER FIRE

This is a poem about how best to face difficulty and disaster in life, and it offers advice that can be of great use to us all. Often our reactions to fear are categorized into two options—fight and flight. And yet here, Deborah Paredez offers us another option. Instead of fleeing, or fighting against whatever forces are bringing us low, we can simply stay where we are and face up to what we have lost.

There is a great deal of dignity in Paredez's poem. The dignity of someone mourning with grace. Someone learning the names of the fallen, in order to honor their loss. Someone tending the wounded, even as the city burns around her. Our losses may be smaller; our forsaken cities or our hearts, or a loved one lost. But we can still approach them in the same spirit: not running away with the mob, but slowly and calmly doing what good we can among the embers.

This may seem counterintuitive. Sometimes our greatest impulse is to follow the herd, and that impulse is particularly strong when it joins forces with our impulse for self-preservation and avoiding pain. And yet to scurry away when things get difficult is a betrayal of oneself, as well as those who have been lost, or who are in pain.

Accepting the difficult parts of our own lives and our own histories can be a very difficult thing to do. And yet it is only by facing up to the fire with dignity and maturity that we can salvage anything from it. So when your city starts to flame, don't run screaming in the other direction. Stand. Watch. Allow yourself to mourn, and eventually to accept the inevitable. But—and this is important—do not forget.

WIFE'S DISASTER MANUAL
Deborah Paredez

When the forsaken city starts to burn,
after the men and children have fled,
stand still, silent as prey, and slowly turn

back. Behold the curse. Stay and mourn
the collapsing doorways, the unbroken bread
in the forsaken city starting to burn.

Don't flinch. Don't join in.
Resist the righteous scurry and instead
stand still, silent as prey. Slowly turn

your thoughts away from escape: the iron
gates unlatched, the responsibilities shed.
When the forsaken city starts to burn,

surrender to your calling, show concern
for those who remain. Come to a dead
standstill. Silent as prey, slowly turn

into something essential. Learn
the names of the fallen. Refuse to run ahead
when the forsaken city starts to burn.
Stand still and silent. Pray. Return.

Condition | Loss of Faith in the World

Also suitable for: DISILLUSIONMENT • NEED FOR INSPIRATION

Sometimes the world can seem overwhelming in its sheer mundanity. We look out upon gray streets, gray skies, and wonder: why can't everything be just a bit more interesting? Most of us lived childhoods suffused with magic, whether it came from Disney or the Brothers Grimm. We believed in Santa, in happy endings, and in the redemptive power of love. Then, we grew up.

If only we lived in the age of miracles, still. If only there were some sign, some evidence, of the miraculous or transcendent. Whether or not we have religion, we all long for a glimpse of something beyond the everyday world that we inhabit. Sometimes that longing can be met through art, or literature, or sheer imagination. But sometimes none of this seems quite enough.

Richard Jones's poem reminds us that miracles don't have to be grand, and they don't have to break the rules of this world that we know so well. Some miracles are small, so small that we don't even think to credit them with the term "miraculous." And yet if we look at them closely enough, we can find just enough magic within them to sustain ourselves.

Sometimes, simply being able to sleep when the winds of misfortune are rattling our windowpanes can be a miracle. Sometimes we can find the miracle in a touch to the hand, a shared glance, a clear sky. There is mystery, and joy, and transcendence woven throughout this dull world of ours, if we only keep our minds open enough to recognize it. The age of miracles never ended. We are living in it right now.

MIRACLES

Richard Jones

I need to witness miracles today—
A river turned to blood,
water become wine,
a burning coal touching the prophet's lips,
black ravens swooping down
to bring a starving man bread and meat,
a poor fisherman raising the dead!
I've heard theologians say
this is not the age of miracles,
but still, I'm easy to impress.
I don't need to climb out of the boat
and walk on water; I'd just like
to put my head on the pillow
while the storm still rages, and rest.

Love and Loss

Condition | Infatuation

Also suitable for: COURTSHIP • FIRST LOVE • UNREQUITED LOVE • ROMANTIC OBSESSION

The beginning of an infatuation is a heady time, during which proportion and propriety both go straight out of the window. If the common attribution of these gorgeous lines to the Persian poet Rumi is correct, then they are many hundreds of years old—and yet they could have been slipped under some lucky lover's door only yesterday. That same longing to know someone inside out, that same lust and fascination we've all felt at the beginning of a truly powerful passion—Rumi knew how to express these things centuries before similar emotions overtook us or even our parents.

Often, we forget the power of this falling feeling once we are out of its clutches, but as soon as it seizes us once more we are reminded of how all-encompassing the start of an obsession can be. When feelings like these are unreciprocated, though, it can be excruciating. Unrequited love is one of those pains suffered by everyone at some point, and yet is no less agonizing for its ubiquity. Nonetheless, however much it may hurt, there is still a beauty to this feeling.

I sometimes meet people in my Poetry Pharmacy who worry that this sort of infatuation will never happen to them again. And yet it tends to be lying just around the corner, waiting for their guard to drop so it can spring. If you are swept up in the longing that Rumi describes, whether or not it is returned, remember that it is something to savor. This is one of the most spectacularly powerful feelings in the world. This is being alive. Don't wish it away—embrace it.

"I WANT TO SEE YOU"
Attributed to Rumi, translator unknown

I want to see you.
Know your voice.

Recognize you when you
first come 'round the corner.

Sense your scent when I come
into a room you've just left.

Know the lift of your heel,
the glide of your foot.

Become familiar with the way
you purse your lips
then let them part,
just the slightest bit,
when I lean in to your space
and kiss you.

I want to know the joy
of how you whisper
"more."

Condition | Unrequited Love

Also suitable for: HEARTBREAK • INFATUATION

Getting someone out of your head can be one of the most dispiriting and time-consuming tasks in life. Little else can be so conflicting. You know you shouldn't be flicking through their profile pictures, or reading through their love letters (depending, probably, on which generation you belong to), but they're already in your head day and night. What harm could it do to indulge yourself?

Often, it can seem as if time, and perhaps a measure of self-restraint, are the only remedies for heartache. Yet Wendy Cope's poem "Two Cures for Love" reminds us that perspective is also a crucial ingredient. Nobody is as perfect as the torrent of chemicals we call "love" can convince us they are. Everyone is flawed; most of us are a little bit pathetic on the inside. The trick is simply to notice this in someone other than yourself.

Humanizing the person you have deified is extremely difficult. How do you pull a god from the heavens, or topple Michelangelo's *David* from his plinth, when you feel diminished and worthless by comparison? All it takes, as Wendy Cope points out in her marvelous and very funny poem, is closer inspection. Knowing someone—even if all that means is coolly contemplating their flaws—is the surest way to undermine their power over you. Of course, laughter can be a great help, too. This poem provides inspiration for both.

TWO CURES FOR LOVE
Wendy Cope

1. Don't see him. Don't phone or write a letter.
2. The easy way: get to know him better.

Condition | Seeking One's Soul Mate

Also suitable for: HEARTBREAK • UNREQUITED LOVE •
MALTREATMENT

All too often in life, we're so consumed by looking for something that we fail to notice we've been absentmindedly swatting it away whenever it came near. This is particularly true when it comes to love. It's an astoundingly bizarre feature of humanity, if we think about it, that we push away the people who want to love us, and instead chase after those who don't want us at all. Why do we do this to ourselves, over and over and over again?

The perfect person could be standing right there, waving at us, holding up a sign that says "True Love This Way"—and yet we'd be completely blind to them. We'd be too busy eyeing up the person sauntering over the horizon, not giving us a second glance. Is the idea of finding the right person really so terrifying it drives us into the arms of someone who's clearly wrong for us? It can certainly seem that way.

The greatest romantic challenge each of us faces is not tracking down that elusive soul mate, or even slimming down until we feel worthy of one. No, our task is far harder. We must find and excise that pernicious part of our psyche that tells us, without our even knowing it, that we should not allow ourselves to be loved exactly as we are. Once you believe that you are worth loving, and that love is worth having, you'll be amazed to discover how many opportunities have been waiting for you, right there, all along.

"YOUR TASK"

Attributed to Rumi, translator unknown

Your task is not to seek for love,
but merely to seek and find all the barriers within yourself
that you have built against it.

Condition | Obsessive Love

Also suitable for: FEAR OF VULNERABILITY • FALLING
IN LOVE • UNREQUITED LOVE

A lot of life is caught up with the obsession and the anguish of love, and sometimes it can be hard to understand why you're tangled up in it at all. The bursts of happiness, the sudden sky-blue clarity of being comfortably in love, can seem to be outweighed utterly by the tumult on either side. It's said that love and madness are not so very far apart. While I don't know about madness, scientists have noted that the profile of the brain in love is strikingly similar to what we expect to find in obsessive-compulsive disorder.

Yet, as Tennyson put it so well:
"'Tis better to have loved and lost
Than never to have loved at all."
Perhaps this will sound trite to the heartsick among you, but it shouldn't. The relentless regret one feels at chances left untaken and mistakes left unmade can be far worse than the brief agony of heartbreak. After all, with a broken heart you know you have tried, and if you have failed you have failed wholeheartedly. Never to have given it a go is a cowardly and quiet way to destroy your own happiness, but it does destroy it nonetheless.

However painful relationships and their endings can be, they're often the only way to evolve as a human being. Being alone is comfortable, but without an antagonist no protagonist would ever develop. We need something to prod us into action, into confronting ourselves frankly. The criticism, acceptance, love, and pain in a relationship do exactly that. And anyway, sometimes we have to celebrate being alive. Give in to the mania. Hold hard. This way at least you live.

THE FIST
Derek Walcott

The fist clenched round my heart
loosens a little, and I gasp
brightness; but it tightens
again. When have I ever not loved
the pain of love? But this has moved

past love to mania. This has the strong
clench of the madman, this is
gripping the ledge of unreason, before
plunging howling into the abyss.

Hold hard then, heart. This way at least you live.

Condition | Love-Hate Relationships

Also suitable for: RELATIONSHIP TURMOIL

What William Carlos Williams captures in this marvelous poem is the complexity of love, the way it thrives on extremes and opposites. Love is not simple—indeed, if it were, how much would we really feel and appreciate it? How much less fascinating love would be if it came without the bite of all those other emotions that are bound up within it.

Williams shows us that love cannot be easily understood. It cannot be distilled down to a single ingredient, or a single motivation. If love were simply passion it would be here one instant, and in the next instant it would be dead. Similarly love cannot be simply pain, or we wouldn't hang on to it as we do. Instead, love is an alloy of all of that anguish, and passion, and joy that we plow into it.

Anyone will tell you that if you stay in a relationship for a lifetime it will involve love, plenty of it, but also a substantial amount of hate. And not just hate, but all its younger siblings, too—doubts, frustrations, annoyances, long silences, and loud clashes. Marriages, or marriagelike commitments, aren't meant to be easy. But if they were, they wouldn't be a challenge, or an achievement.

But I think we can take something from this poem to make the challenge easier to overcome. What Williams shows us so beautifully here is that the pain and the difficulty isn't inimical to love; it is intrinsic to it. Without pain there would be no love for us at all. Instead of running away from the difficulties of love, or taking them as evidence that the relationship isn't meant to be, we can comfort ourselves with the idea that pain is the yang to passion's yin. And as in any marriage, it is through their opposition that they find balance.

LOVE
William Carlos Williams

Love is twain, it is not single,
Gold and silver mixed to one,
Passion 'tis and pain which mingle
Glist'ring then for aye undone.

Pain it is not; wondering pity
Dies or e'er the pang is fled;
Passion 'tis not, foul and gritty,
Born one instant, instant dead.

Love is twain, it is not single,
Gold and silver mixed to one,
Passion 'tis and pain which mingle
Glist'ring then for aye undone.

Condition | One-Sided Love

Also suitable for: CRUSHES • CREATIVE INSPIRATION

One-sided love. That strange, elated agony will be familiar to most of us; indeed, unrequited love tends to be the first taste of romantic love that any of us experiences. But whether you're a teenager pining in your bedroom, or a grown adult still longing for what you can't have, the pain is still the same. And so is the inspiration.

I think it was Yeats who said, "Only an aching heart conceives a changeless work of art." Love's tribulations are what leads to the finest human expression: the most memorable, perhaps the most anguished, but ultimately the art that will endure—the art that will touch people in the same place that you are hurting right now; and that might just show them the beauty in their pain.

And although it's true that heartbreak can be the impetus for dazzling works of creativity, the work of art doesn't have to be an epic poem, or a masterpiece fit for a gallery. It could simply be a prompt toward self-examination, the push we need to really look at ourselves and ask, "What is it that I'm looking for? What is it about this person that I think I need so terribly?"

Not all love is selfless. In fact, it seldom is, at least at the beginning. What this poem shows us is that sometimes we love not because we need to be loved back, but because we need to love for its own sake. Often, we fall for others because we see something in them that we need in our own life; or at least that we think we need. Examining this urge can help us to find those patches of emptiness within ourselves and our lives, and perhaps to find new, healthier ways to fill them. Ways that don't rely on another person.

SOMETIMES WITH ONE I LOVE
Walt Whitman

Sometimes with one I love I fill myself with rage for fear I effuse
    unreturn'd love,
But now I think there is no unreturn'd love, the pay is certain
    one way or another,
(I loved a certain person ardently and my love was not return'd,
Yet out of that I have written these songs.)

Condition | False Expectations in Love

Also suitable for: BREAKUPS • DISAPPOINTMENT •
DISILLUSIONMENT

When the rose-tinted glasses come off in a relationship, that can often be the end of it. You allow your disappointment in the other person to poison your idea of them completely, even though they may have had no idea of the standards they were supposed to be living up to. Meanwhile, they feel insecure and exposed, wondering where the light of adoration has gone from your eyes. Something, however trivial it might have been, has destroyed the person you loved—and yet, as far as they're concerned, they're the same person they were yesterday.

We look to our relationships to fix us: to plug the gaps we sense in our own psyches, and to heal us in all the places we've been hurt. But this weight of expectation is too huge to be carried by any one person—any real person, that is. Instead, we construct elaborate characters to play out the dramas in our heads. Our minds cloud with optimism and naivete, until the love affair we are having is as much with ourselves—with the phantoms conjured by our own imaginations—as it is with someone else.

There are few things more painful than being disappointed by someone you think you know. But there are also few things more wonderful than being loved for who you really are. If we allow ourselves to project our own desires onto those we love, then disappointment in them is inevitable. When we manage to take the rose-tinted spectacles off, that's when real love begins.

DEFINING THE PROBLEM
Wendy Cope

I can't forgive you. Even if I could,
You wouldn't pardon me for seeing through you.
And yet I cannot cure myself of love
For what I thought you were before I knew you.

Condition | Rocky Relationships

Also suitable for: HEARTBREAK • PRIDE • BICKERING IN
RELATIONSHIPS • SULKING

Anyone who's been in a relationship knows that moment: you're in a sulk, and there are two voices in your head. One of them is cold, angry, and triumphant at causing your partner pain. The other voice is quieter, more confused. It gently wishes that none of this had happened, that you could go back to the way things were before the sulk. It doesn't really understand why things have become so unpleasant, or why this standoff is important. The tragedy is that, so often, it's the first of these voices that is listened to.

Once you and your partner are deeply entrenched in a sulk, you'll often find that neither of you can remotely recall who began it or why. Somehow this makes the situation worse: you can't remember what was said, but you know for sure that you're in the right. Even if one of you wanted to apologize, they wouldn't know what to apologize for.

And then come those heartbreakingly sad moments described by P. K. Page in "Cross," when one of you tries to make peace, and the other realizes only after rejecting the advance that peace is really all they want, too. Sometimes, in refusing to forgive someone else, we are actually trying to delay the moment when they forgive us, and we must admit to ourselves that we have done something wrong.

We have all been on either side of this equation. We have all made the wrong choices before, and hated the consequences. And that is why we know, deep down, what we need to do when the sulk sets in. Being bighearted, forgiving, and loving is better than being right. Having someone to hold you is better than winning. Keep reaching out, and your partner will eventually reach back. If you find yourself in this situation, perhaps try reading them P. K. Page's poem. Peace is worth more than pride.

CROSS
P. K. Page

He has leaned for hours against the veranda railing
gazing the darkened garden out of mind
while she with battened hatches rides out the wind
that will blow for a year or a day, there is no telling.

As to why they are cross she barely remembers now.
That they are cross, she is certain. They hardly speak.
Feel cold and hurt and stony. For a week
have without understanding behaved so.

And will continue so to behave for neither
can come to that undemanded act of love—
kiss the sleeping princess or sleep with the frog—
and break the spell which holds them each from the other.

Or if one ventures towards it, the other, shy,
dissembles, regrets too late the dissimulation
and sits, hands slack, heart tiny, the hard solution
having again passed by.

Silly the pair of them. Yet they make me weep.
Two on a desert island, back to back
who, while the alien world howls round them black
go their own ways, fall emptily off to sleep.

Condition | Romantic Boredom

Also suitable for: LACK OF EXCITEMENT IN LOVE • LONGING
FOR ROMANCE

So much of what we read about love describes the passion, the anguish, the soaring highs and searing lows. But that's not the whole story. This is a poem about the real business of love, once all the Romeo and Juliet drama has been finished with. This is a poem about the realities of a happily ever after.

Often, in my Poetry Pharmacy, the poems I prescribe aren't about comforting people at all. What people need more than comfort is to be given a different perspective on their inner turmoil. They need to reframe their narrative in a way that leaves room for happiness and gratitude. When we take our loved ones for granted, when we diminish them because they're not glamorous enough, or spontaneous enough, or exciting enough, what we really need is a new way of appreciating the unremarkable elements of love.

Somebody once said to me that love is like an old-fashioned long-playing record, and thoughtlessness, betrayal, and unkindness are the equivalent of moving the needle back to the beginning. Do that enough times, and you'll find you never get to hear the end. Love may begin with a fanfare of trumpets and crash of cymbals, but any record needs nuance if it's going to remain a pleasure to listen to. The lulls are just as precious as the upswings. If you listen to your love like a connoisseur, you might find that you no longer pine for the drama of the opening bars.

U. A. Fanthorpe reminds us that, in the end, a lifetime of love and support and kindness—of the steady, gentle sort—is far more meaningful than the bright sparks of passion. Because isn't every hinge oiled and every drain unblocked really a love token? Who would have roses, when they could have someone who takes care of the road tax?

ATLAS

U. A. Fanthorpe

There is a kind of love called maintenance,
Which stores the WD40 and knows when to use it;

Which checks the insurance, and doesn't forget
The milkman; which remembers to plant bulbs;

Which answers letters; which knows the way
The money goes; which deals with dentists

And Road Fund Tax and meeting trains,
And postcards to the lonely; which upholds

The permanently rickety elaborate
Structures of living; which is Atlas.

And maintenance is the sensible side of love,
Which knows what time and weather are doing
To my brickwork; insulates my faulty wiring;
Laughs at my dryrotten jokes; remembers
My need for gloss and grouting; which keeps
My suspect edifice upright in air,
As Atlas did the sky.

Condition | Complacency in Love

Also suitable for: SKEWED PRIORITIES • LOW SELF-ESTEEM • SELF-LOATHING • UNAPPRECIATIVENESS

Love is a very hard thing to pin down or define. In fact, as countless books and films have told us, it's easy to be in love without even realizing it. Love comes and goes; it baffles everyone it touches. How then could something so flimsy, so ephemeral, be the motivating force of human life? It can be easy to feel we are becoming indifferent to it, and to get complacent.

And yet, like the speaker of Edna St. Vincent Millay's sonnet "Love is not all," we prove time and again that love is more dear to us than anything else. We value the love that we feel more than we value our own lives. After all, as this poem leaves us asking ourselves, would you sell your memories of a loved one for food, or for medicine? Would you stop loving someone, if you could, to save yourself from starvation? I suspect not.

Not the least part of love's at times confounding importance in human lives is its disregard for material things. It is one of very few resources that are available equally to rich and to poor, to the weak and the strong. We all know the cliché of the billionaire who would give everything up if only his lost love would come back to him. Those of us who have love are, in a very real way, richer than he is.

I would add, though, that it is not only the sheer value of love for others that we need to recognize and remember, but also of love for ourselves—above all when we are in our deepest depths. Frequently, when we are feeling at our gloomiest, it is because we have forgotten our capacity for loving those around us; and that forgetting, all too often, stems from an initial loss of self-love. Hold on to both, and we'll find that everything else is a lot less important than it seems.

"LOVE IS NOT ALL"

Edna St. Vincent Millay

Love is not all: it is not meat nor drink
Nor slumber nor a roof against the rain;
Nor yet a floating spar to men that sink
And rise and sink and rise and sink again;
Love can not fill the thickened lung with breath,
Nor clean the blood, nor set the fractured bone;
Yet many a man is making friends with death
Even as I speak, for lack of love alone.
It well may be that in a difficult hour,
Pinned down by pain and moaning for release,
Or nagged by want past resolution's power,
I might be driven to sell your love for peace,
Or trade the memory of this night for food.
It well may be. I do not think I would.

Condition | Losing the Spark

Also suitable for: BECOMING BORED OR BORING • FALLING OUT OF LOVE • ROCKY RELATIONSHIPS

Ann Sansom's poem "Voice" is for people whose relationships are floundering, who don't understand why their partner seems to be becoming tired of them. They were hanging on your every word at the beginning, and now they seem to greet you with an inner sigh every time you open your mouth. How fickle they must be; how insincere!

In truth, of course, the fault in relationships is almost never one-sided. The lesson of this poem is that sometimes just pouring out your heart, burdening your lover with all your troubles and your woes and your neediness, isn't the best way to remain attractive. If, every time you get home, you start to complain about work, or how nobody seems to appreciate you, or about that itchy skin condition you just can't get rid of, you might find that you start to lose some of the mystery.

Naturally, you want to be in a mutually supportive relationship. It's important that your partner knows you trust them, and it's equally important for you to have someone to go to when things actually get bad. But that doesn't mean your partner is obliged to care about the trivial gripes they know you wouldn't inflict on a friend. After all, no one wants to feel like their partner's dumping ground.

As important as it is—and as difficult as it can be—to make ourselves vulnerable in a relationship, we often forget that what originally attracted our partners to us may have been the twinkle in our eye, our coolness, our slight distance. There's no contradiction in keeping a relationship fresh and exciting while still being emotionally available to one another. Whatever the therapists may say, sometimes talking about it isn't the answer at all.

VOICE
Ann Sansom

Call by all means, but just once
don't use the *broken heart again* voice;
the *I'm sick to death of life and women
and romance* voice *but with a little help
I'll try to struggle on* voice

Spare me the promise and the curse
voice, the ansafoney *Call me, please
when you get in* voice, the *nobody knows
the trouble I've seen* voice; the *I'd value
your advice* voice.

I want the how it was voice;
the *call me irresponsible but aren't I nice* voice;
the *such a bastard but I warn them in advance* voice.
The *We all have weaknesses
and mine is being wicked* voice

the *life's short and wasting time's
the only vice* voice, the *stay in touch,
but out of reach* voice. I want to hear
the *things it's better not to broach* voice
the *things it's wiser not to voice* voice.

Condition | Heartbreak

Also suitable for: BREAKUPS • ROMANTIC OBSESSION • OVERREACTION TO LOSS

Duncan Forbes's "Recension Day" is not the sort of poem that is going to envelop you in feelings of warmth, hope, and possibility. Sometimes, poems like that do no good at all. When your heart is broken, there's no point presuming that one simple thought, one simple, beautiful poem, will undo the anguish. The problem with anguish is that it comes in unpredictable tides. One moment, you may be surviving, even happy—the next, the current has caught you and you're swimming for your life. The journey from the bleakness of heartbreak to full recovery is long and arduous, and it is far from straight.

One element of the grief associated with love is facing up to the absolute enormity of loss. There is nothing trivial about true heartbreak: it is a sort of grief, because something that had been fundamental to your life until that moment has died. This poem is one of the most profound expressions of that feeling. Sometimes, in the process of grieving, what you need is not comfort but for someone to show you that they've felt the same way. They endured. They were not mad. But it was not easy for them either.

The wisest people know that the fact something happens to everyone does not somehow invalidate its agony. Pain is pain, whether it is unique or universal. Too often, when we are suffering, the wound is only deepened by our sense that we are not entitled to our misery. We are overreacting, we are told: we are being dramatic—perhaps we are allowing ourselves to wallow. Sometimes, all we really need is for someone to give us permission to feel as we feel. That is what this poem does so well.

RECENSION DAY
Duncan Forbes

Unburn the boat, rebuild the bridge,
Reconsecrate the sacrilege,
Unspill the milk, decry the tears,
Turn back the clock, relive the years,
Replace the smoke inside the fire,
Unite fulfilment with desire,
Undo the done, gainsay the said,
Revitalise the buried dead,
Revoke the penalty and clause,
Reconstitute unwritten laws,
Repair the heart, untie the tongue,
Change faithless old to hopeful young,
Inure the body to disease
And help me to forget you please.

Condition | Divorce

Divorce can be especially painful because it feels like it proves its participants wrong. You were optimistic about your love and what it could withstand; now you see that that optimism was unfounded. This sense of having been foolish, of having wasted one's time or been deceived, is particularly agonizing in the wake of losing someone you love, or once loved.

But Jack Gilbert's poem "Failing and Flying" says something simple and intuitive that makes all the difference. Your marriage wasn't a mistake, and the efforts you put into it weren't wasted. Every happy moment that relationship brought you was a success. The simple fact that it's finished doesn't mean it wasn't worth pursuing, or that it didn't help to shape you into someone wiser. Sometimes, there comes a point where a marriage has served its purpose. It will be more of a success if it finishes then, instead of limping on into eternity.

Undying love is a wonderful idea, but both it and the institution of marriage were conceived back when average life expectancies were much lower than they are now. These days you can expect to spend fifty, sixty, even seventy years with your spouse. It's a very particular, very hardy sort of love that can march over those great distances: one which is not necessarily better or worse than any other kind, but which is certainly rare. When we look back over our lives, there are golden moments: honeymoons in Provence, years in a particularly lovely job, or just periods when everything seemed to be going our way. These flashes of glory are impermanent, but by God are they worth having. If we can manage to see a finished relationship or a dissolved marriage as one of these moments—finite, but precious and gleaming in our memories— then we will have neither fallen nor failed.

FAILING AND FLYING
Jack Gilbert

Everyone forgets that Icarus also flew.
It's the same when love comes to an end,
or the marriage fails and people say
they knew it was a mistake, that everybody
said it would never work. That she was
old enough to know better. But anything
worth doing is worth doing badly.
Like being there by that summer ocean
on the other side of the island while
love was fading out of her, the stars
burning so extravagantly those nights that
anyone could tell you they would never last.
Every morning she was asleep in my bed
like a visitation, the gentleness in her
like antelope standing in the dawn mist.
Each afternoon I watched her coming back
through the hot stony field after swimming,
the sea light behind her and the huge sky
on the other side of that. Listened to her
while we ate lunch. How can they say
the marriage failed? Like the people who
came back from Provence (when it was Provence)
and said it was pretty but the food was greasy.
I believe Icarus was not failing as he fell,
but just coming to the end of his triumph.

Condition | Bereavement

Also suitable for: EXTREME GRIEF • MOURNING

Dealing with the death of a person you relied on is one of the toughest challenges any of us ever face. Such grief can be even more overwhelming than that caused by a broken heart, particularly when death comes without warning—or comes to a parent. It's a double blow: you are being stripped of the very person whose support could have helped you to deal with their own terrible absence in your life.

I remember very clearly something my late father said to me when he was dying: it has kept me company through the decades I've been without him. "When I'm gone," he said, "'you'll still hear my voice. It's just that it won't annoy you anymore."

This was a brilliant thing to say. When you've lost someone, it's easy to imagine that they've literally been lost. They're gone, and that's it: they no longer exist. It's a feeling like being robbed, or emptied. But anyone who's come out the other side of grief—and believe me, you will come out the other side, though you'll never forget it—knows that it's not like that. If someone has had an influence on your life, if they've helped to shape your personality, then they'll remain there for you. They'll remain there in you.

This isn't to deny death, it's just to look at it in a different light. Your lover, or your parent, or the child you've lost—they may not be physically present, but their memory and their voice remain. They are still out there somewhere, scattered among all the beautiful things on the earth, like the voice in Mary Elizabeth Frye's "Do Not Stand at My Grave and Weep." This poem, and the wisdom it imparts, can change a sense of loss into a sense of hope.

DO NOT STAND AT MY GRAVE AND WEEP
Mary Elizabeth Frye

Do not stand at my grave and weep,
I am not there; I do not sleep.
I am a thousand winds that blow,
I am the diamond glints on snow,
I am the sun on ripened grain,
I am the gentle autumn rain.
When you awaken in the morning's hush
I am the swift uplifting rush
Of quiet birds in circling flight.
I am the soft starlight at night.
Do not stand at my grave and cry,
I am not there; I did not die.

Condition | Balanced Grief

Also suitable for: NUMBNESS IN THE FACE OF LOSS • UNDER- OR OVERREACTION TO LOSS

I often come across people in my pharmacies who are grieving, but who can't quite understand why their whole world hasn't been destroyed. Why are they still able to function? Why is life still the same in so many important ways? Is their reaction somehow wrong? The answer is that these people have a balanced grief, the kind of grief we would all wish for our loved ones. And yet somehow the great hysteria surrounding death has led them to believe that they are being callous, or uncaring.

On the other hand, the immensity of death—its permanence and inescapability—can lead us to deify the departed. As a society, we are deeply uncomfortable with death: we push it to the outskirts of our lives, euphemize it, deny its approach. This makes us more comfortable during the good times, but it can also make grief all the more baffling when it looms up to surprise us. We are tempted to idolize those we've lost: to deny their flaws and ultimately their humanity itself. Perhaps this makes it easier to separate ourselves from them.

In Wendy Cope's poem "My Funeral" we hear a very human, somewhat flawed, and yet deeply reassuring voice from beyond. There's no need to make a scene, it says; no need to grandstand and get caught up in the drama of it all. Give your reading, sing your song, but don't allow yourself to wallow. Get on with life. No one will be scoring you on how desolate you appear.

After all, the deceased won't have gone anywhere. She'll still be here in your mind, tutting when you start to hog the limelight or looking pointedly at her watch if you overrun your five minutes. She's not a saint and never will be—instead, she's just the same imperfect person you loved before, and whom you love still. Deeply, of course, but within measure.

MY FUNERAL
Wendy Cope

I hope I can trust you, friends, not to use our relationship
As an excuse for an unsolicited ego-trip.
I have seen enough of them at funerals and they make
    me cross.
At this one, though deceased, I aim to be the boss.
If you are asked to talk about me for five minutes, please do
    not go on for eight.
There is a strict timetable at the crematorium and nobody
    wants to be late.
If invited to read a poem, just read the bloody poem.
    If requested
To sing a song, just sing it, as suggested,
And don't say anything. Though I will not be there,
Glancing pointedly at my watch and fixing the speaker with a
    malevolent stare,
Remember that this was how I always reacted
When I felt that anybody's speech, sermon or poetry reading
    was becoming too protracted.
Yes, I was impatient and intolerant, and not always polite
And if there aren't many people at my funeral, it will serve
    me right.

Condition | Maturing Grief

Also suitable for: DESPAIR • HEARTBREAK • LOSS

Elizabeth Jennings's poem "Into the Hour" is about a time that you may not believe in right now if you are mired in grief. It's the moment when, unexpectedly and for no very clear reason, you discover that the worst is over. To begin with, when you're starting to make sense of loss, it seems completely impenetrable. You feel a great weight of madness, confusion, and anger. It's hard to imagine what it will be like to recover; hard to believe that time will ever come.

And yet, of course, it does come. There will be a moment when you find it easy to reach out and take other people's hands, both literally and figuratively. There will be a moment when you feel that the world around you is looking at you with kindness. You will become aware of the possibilities of life, and of new love, and know that you are healing.

Grief is surgery. It consumes you, for a while; it puts you under. But once your scars have knitted together, you realize that all that pain was necessary. It is a healing process, despite the fact that it must begin with violence.

This poem reminds us that there is hope, and there is resolution. Whether you're grieving over a love affair or the death of a person, you will get better. Grief will flower into new love. Just wait—you'll see.

INTO THE HOUR
Elizabeth Jennings

I have come into the hour of a white healing.
Grief's surgery is over and I wear
The scar of my remorse and of my feeling.

I have come into a sudden sunlit hour
When ghosts are scared to corners. I have come
Into the time when grief begins to flower

Into a new love. It had filled my room
Long before I recognized it. Now
I speak its name. Grief finds its good way home.

The apple-blossom's handsome on the bough
And Paradise spreads round. I touch its grass.
I want to celebrate but don't know how.

I need not speak though everyone I pass
Stares at me kindly. I would put my hand
Into their hands. Now I have lost my loss

In some way I may later understand.
I hear the singing of the summer grass.
And love, I find, has no considered end,

Nor is it subject to the wilderness
Which follows death. I am not traitor to
A person or a memory. I trace

Behind that love another which is running
Around, ahead. I need not ask its meaning.

Condition | Loss of Elderly Relatives

Also suitable for: DEATH IN OLD AGE • FEAR OF MORTALITY

Death and misery are now so strongly linked together in the popular imagination that the two are difficult to separate. We've reached a point where we can't think about death in any other terms. And yet dying does not always need to be met with grief and horror. Often, to those who are taken by death, it can be a great relief.

In Paul Durcan's poem, Auntie Maureen, aged ninety-four, thinks this is a glorious morning to die. And why shouldn't she? Like many other people who have lived full lives and then watched them grow gradually emptier with age, she is ready for this next step. She is smiling, and calm, and keen to share the happy news of her passing with anyone who'll listen—in this case, her nephew Paul.

Death, in the right circumstances, can be a blessing. A life lived well, and to its maximum, has come to its natural conclusion. Auntie Maureen can float above her life now, and see it as a completed story. Isn't that something worth smiling about? And if Auntie Maureen can greet her end so cheerfully, and with such equanimity, would it not be rather rude of us to go around being miserable about it? There are some deaths, some very fortunate deaths, which do not call for grief. They demand celebration.

MAUREEN DURCAN
Paul Durcan

A grain of sand I am blown on to a
Clump of heather and I see
Alight large above me a butterfly
With black and orange stripes—
It's Auntie Maureen aged ninety-four
Smiling down upon me
And she is saying
"While you were sleeping, Paul, I died.
Isn't it the most glorious morning!"

WHAT ARE THE POEMS THAT MEAN
THE MOST TO YOU?

If they're not in this book, William would love to hear about them. Email him at william@thepoetrypharmacy.com.

INDEX OF FIRST LINES

INDEX OF CONDITIONS

ACKNOWLEDGMENTS

The editors and publisher gratefully acknowledge the following for permission to reprint copyright material:

MAYA ANGELOU: "Phenomenal Woman" and "Still I Rise" from *And Still I Rise: A Book of Poems,* copyright © Maya Angelou, 1978. Used by permission of Random House, an imprint and division of Penguin Random House LLC. All rights reserved. Any third party use of this material, outside of this publication, is prohibited. Interested parties must apply direct to Penguin Random House LLC for permission.

WENDELL BERRY: "The Peace of Wild Things" from *New Collected Poems,* Counterpoint, 2012, copyright © Wendell Berry, 2012. Reprinted by permission of Counterpoint Press.

ELIZABETH BISHOP: "One Art" from *Poems,* copyright © The Alice H. Methfessel Trust, 2011. Reprinted with the permission of Farrar, Straus and Giroux.

JOHN BURNSIDE: "Of Gravity and Light" ("enlightenment") from *The Light Trap* published by Jonathan Cape, copyright © 2002. Reprinted by permission of The Random House Group Limited.

JULIA DARLING: "Chemotherapy" from *Sudden Collapses in Public Places*, Arc Publications, 2003. Reprinted by permission of the publisher.

IMTIAZ DHARKER: "Front Door" from *I Speak for the Devil*, Bloodaxe Books, 2011. Reprinted by permission of Bloodaxe Books, www.bloodaxebooks.com.

MARK DOTY: "Golden Retrievals" from *Sweet Machine*, Jonathan Cape, 1998, copyright © Mark Doty, 1998. Reprinted by permission of HarperCollins Publishers and the author.

PAUL DURCAN: "Maureen Durcan" from *Praise in which I live and move and have my being*, Harvill Secker, copyright © 2012. Reproduced by permission of The Random House Group Limited.

U. A. FANTHORPE: "Atlas" from *Selected Poems*, Enitharmon Press, 2013. Reprinted by kind permission of Dr. R.V. Bailey.

HELEN FARISH: "Look at These" from *Intimates*, published by Jonathan Cape, copyright © 2003. Reprinted by permission of The Random House Group Limited.

VICKI FEAVER: "Ironing" from *The Handless Maiden*, published by Jonathan Cape, copyright © 1994. Reprinted by permission of The Random House Group Ltd.

JAMES FENTON: "The Ideal" and "The Mistake" from *Yellow Tulips: Poems 1968–2011*, Faber & Faber, 2012, copyright © James Fenton, 2012. Reprinted by permission of United Agents LLP and the author James Fenton.

DUNCAN FORBES: "Recension Day" from *Taking Liberties*, Enitharmon Press, 1993. Reprinted by permission of the publisher.

THE POETRY PHARMACY

William Sieghart has had a long career in publishing and the arts. He established the Forward Prizes for Poetry in 1992 and founded the UK's National Poetry Day in 1994. He is a former chairman of the Arts Council Lottery Panel and current chairman of Forward Thinking, a charity seeking peace in the Middle East; the Somerset House Trust; and StreetSmart, Action for the Homeless. His previous anthologies include *Winning Words: Inspiring Poems for Everyday Life* (2014), *Poems of the Decade: An Anthology of the Forward Books of Poetry* (2015), and *100 Prized Poems: Twenty-five Years of the Forward Books* (2016). He was awarded a CBE in the 2016 New Year Honours for services to public libraries. His Poetry Pharmacy began in 2014; since then he has prescribed almost a thousand poems up and down the UK, over hundreds of hours of in-person consultations.